My debt to history is one which
cannot be calculated. I know of no other
motivation which so accounts for my
awakening interest as a young lad in the
principles of leadership and government. . . .
I know that the one great external influence
which, more than anything else,
nourished and sustained that interest in
government and public service was the endless
reading of history which I began as a boy
and which I have kept up ever since.

HARRY TRUMAN

The unparalleled rise of America
has not been the result of riches in lands,
forests, or mines; it sprang from
the ideas and ideals which liberated minds
and stimulated the spirits of men.
In those ideas and ideals are the soul
of the people. No American can
review this vast pageant of progress without
confidence and faith, without courage, strength,
and resolution for the future.

HERBERT HOOVER

Kennedy: "A Nation of Immigrants," New York, 1959
Eisenhower: Reader's Digest, October, 1948
Truman: "Memoirs," © 1955, Time Inc.
Hoover: 150th anniversary address, Yorktown, Va., October 19, 1931

Important Dates and Events to Remember
1675-1774

1675 Expanding New England settlements cut into Indian territory and arouse anger of tribes. Bad feeling erupts in King Philip's War (1675-1678).

1676 Bacon's Rebellion. In Virginia, tobacco planters organize a military force led by Nathaniel Bacon, after Governor Sir William Berkeley refuses to protect them from Indian raids. Berkeley calls the planters "rebels" and moves troops against them. Fighting is indecisive, but rebellion shows free men will act to gain equal protection under law.

1704 February, French and Indians attack Deerfield, Massachusetts, killing or capturing 165 settlers.
News-Letter, first regularly issued newspaper in America, founded in Boston.

1706 January 6, Ben Franklin born in Boston.

1716 First theater in America is built in Williamsburg, Virginia.

1718 Pirates, driven out of Bahamas by English fleet, make final stand on coast of Carolinas. Threat ends with death of Blackbeard and Stede Bonnet.
San Antonio (Texas) founded by Spanish. *Rancheros* establish first cattle herds.

1720 "Mississippi Bubble" bursts when John Law's claims of riches in Louisiana prove to be false. Thousands of French investors are ruined.

1731 First circulating library in America begun by Ben Franklin in Philadelphia.

1732 February 22, George Washington born at Bridges Creek, Virginia.
Franklin publishes *Poor Richard's Almanack* (1732-1757).
James Oglethorpe given charter for Georgia colony, makes it refuge for debtors imprisoned in England.

1735 August, John Peter Zenger, editor of New York *Weekly Journal,* tried on charge of libeling Governor William Cosby. Defense attorney Andrew Hamilton pleads the right of men to write and speak their minds, wins victory for Zenger and for freedom of press in America.

1741 Vitus Jonassen Bering discovers Alaska on second voyage, commissioned by Russian empress, to find a link between continents of Asia and North America.

1742 Oglethorpe saves Georgia and South Carolina from Spanish conquest by tricking an invasion fleet of 36 ships and defeating attacking force.

1749 British send Protestant soldiers to settle in Nova Scotia, demand that Catholic Acadians living there sign oath of allegiance to Britain or lose their property.

1753 George Washington, on orders of Governor Dinwiddie of Virginia, warns the commander of French outposts along the Ohio River to stop invading British territory.

1754 May, first battle of French and Indian War (1754-1763) won by George Washington, who defeats French near Great Meadows, Pennsylvania.
July 3, Washington surrenders Fort Necessity to French.

1755 General Edward Braddock defeated and mortally wounded by French and Indians in ambush near Fort Du Quesne, Pennsylvania. Washington is present at the battle.
British seize Acadians' land and banish them to other colonies. Event later becomes the theme of Longfellow's poem *Evangeline*.

1757 William Pitt, the "Great Commoner," rises to power in England and promises the colonies a voice in the government, and troops and money to fight the war.

1758 July, General James Abercrombie, new British commander, defeated by the Marquis de Montcalm in battle at Fort Ticonderoga, New York.
November, French defeat at Fort Du Quesne, which British rename Fort Pitt, returns Ohio Valley to Britain.

1759 September, 5,000 British troops under General James Wolfe scale cliffs to the Plains of Abraham, overlooking Quebec, and win the city. Wolfe and French commander, Montcalm, are killed.

1760 George III becomes king of England.

1761 "Writs of assistance," permitting royal agents to enter colonial homes and businesses to collect taxes, anger Americans.

1763 French and Indian War ends with Treaty of Paris. Britain now claims half the North American continent. Pontiac, chief of the Ottawas, leads Indian revolt. Fighting is violent and destructive until Pontiac is killed and uprising crushed.

1764 "No taxation without representation," the colonists cry after Parliament declares it has the right to tax Americans even though they are not represented in the House of Commons.

1765 March, Stamp Act places a tax on newspapers, legal documents, other papers. Sons of Liberty, secret organization of patriots, spring up in colonies to resist enforcement of the act.
May, Patrick Henry attacks Stamp Act in Virginia House of Burgesses.

1766 Stamp Act repealed with support of William Pitt. Americans rejoice.

1767 New attempts to enforce taxes are supported by soldiers shipped from England to New York City. Citizens and soldiers clash.
June, New York Assembly forbidden to meet until New Yorkers show a "respectful" attitude toward royal troops.

1768 British soldiers arrive in Boston.

1770 March 5, Boston Massacre. British soldiers, stoned by Bostonians, fire on crowd, kill 3, wound 8.

1772 British schooner *Gaspee*, sent to Narragansett Bay to enforce collection of taxes, is burned by Providence citizens.

1773 December 16, Boston Tea Party. In protest against tea taxed without their consent, Americans board English ships in Boston harbor at night and dump tea cargo into bay.

1774 June, George III orders the port of Boston closed to punish the colonists. Twelve of the 13 colonies send 56 delegates to the First Continental Congress in Philadelphia in September to discuss what steps to take against Britain.

The question before the court and you, gentlemen of the jury, is not of small nor private concern, it is not the cause of a poor printer, nor of New York alone, which you are now trying. No! It may in its consequence affect every freeman that lives under a British government on the Main of America. It is the best cause. It is the cause of liberty; and I make no doubt but your upright conduct this day will not only entitle you to love and esteem of your fellow citizens; but every man who prefers freedom to a life of slavery will bless and honor you as men who have baffled the attempt of tyranny, and, by an impartial and uncorrupt verdict, have laid a noble foundation for securing to ourselves, our posterity, and our neighbors that to which nature and the laws of our country have given us a right—the liberty both of exposing and opposing arbitrary power (in these parts of the world, at least) by speaking and writing truth."

(Quoted from Hamilton's own "Brief Narrative of the Case and Tryal of John Peter Zenger" [New York, 1736])

THE GOLDEN BOOK

HISTORY of the UNITED STATES

by **EARL SCHENCK MIERS**

LITT. B., M.A., L.H.D.

VOLUME 2

THE INDIAN WARS

Paintings by **ALTON S. TOBEY**

Drawings by **RICHARD P. KLUGA**

Technical Consultants:
L. ETHAN ELLIS AND RICHARD M. BROWN
of the Department of History, Rutgers University

HERBERT J. SANBORN, *Art Research*

GOLDEN PRESS **NEW YORK**

How To Use This Volume THE INDIAN WARS tells of the battles
the American settlers had in the years between 1675 and 1774. It may be read
from cover to cover. It discusses many events that took place over a long span of
time. The events taken up in each chapter are described briefly at the opening of
the chapter and also on the contents page. This will allow the reader to find any
subject he wants quickly and easily. Each section of the text also has the dates
of the period it covers printed in blue at the top of the page. The principal events
and the dates on which they occurred are listed in the timetable on the inside
front cover. Maps are included throughout the text, and also on the inside back
cover. An index for the entire series is contained in Volume X.

ONTENTS ~ THE INDIAN WARS

Library of Congress Catalog Card Number: 63-9433
© copyright 1963 by Golden Press, Inc. and The Ridge Press, Inc. Printed in the U.S.A. by Western Printing and Lithographing Co.

Designed and produced by
The Ridge Press, Inc.
17 East 45th Street, New York, N. Y.

BLOODY DAYS IN NEW ENGLAND

*Pushed off their hunting grounds,
the Indians strike back at the settlers
in King Philip's War.*

For nearly forty years New Englanders had lived in peace with the Indians. Now and then a small dispute arose, but it was quickly settled. There were about 4,000 "praying Indians"—Indians who had been converted to Christianity. The red man had learned to live without raids and scalpings —or so New Englanders believed.

Each year the English had pushed their settlements and trading posts deeper into Indian hunting grounds, both to the north and the west. Meanwhile, Dutch traders at Albany and wandering French traders had supplied the Indians with firearms. The tomahawk and fire arrow had been no match for a gun, but with the weapons they had bought, the Indians believed they could meet the white invaders on even terms.

Thus did King Philip talk to his Wampanoags in Rhode Island, and later to the Nipmucks and Narragansetts. He told the Indians that they had the power to save their favorite fishing and hunting grounds. And he stirred up their feelings until they shouted with anger at the white man. When in June, 1675, a settler in Swansea, Rhode Island, shot an Indian who had been seen looting houses, King Philip's War exploded upon New England. Before the fighting ended, it had left a long and bloody trail from Massachusetts to the frontier settlements of Connecticut.

CAPTURE OF MARY ROWLANDSON

Typical of the savage assaults that King Philip's warriors struck against town after town was the attack on Lancaster, a settlement on the Massachusetts frontier. Mary White Rowlandson later told how the popping of guns was heard as the Indians came howling out of the forest at about sunrise on February 10, 1676. Her minister husband was in Boston on business that day and she faced the trouble alone. From the window she looked out on frightful scenes: houses afire with the smoke rising in thick columns, a child knocked on the head and killed, a man shot running toward his barn, Indians climbing onto rooftops to shoot down into the town's fortifications.

Then the Indians rushed to the house where Mary was hiding and set it on fire. She tried to escape, with the baby in her arms and her small son and daughter cling-

ing to her skirt. But "the Indians shot so thick that the bullets rattled against the house as if one had taken a handful of stones and threw them." Indians with guns, spears, and hatchets were on every side. Both Mary and her baby were wounded before the Indians seized her.

That night the Indians and their captives camped on a hill overlooking the ruins of Lancaster. While the hungry captives huddled together, the Indians shouted, danced, and feasted in celebration of their victory. Next morning they marched northward and snow added to the misery of the captives. On the ninth night, Mary's baby died.

Mary White Rowlandson was held prisoner by the Indians until the English ransomed her.

Mary was sold into slavery to a sachem (chief), who in turn sold her to a Narragansett Indian. Her daughter, she learned, had been sold into slavery by a "praying Indian." The price: one gun. No one would tell what had happened to her son.

For the first week of captivity Mary ate almost nothing. The second week, weakened by hunger, she tried to swallow "the filthy trash" the Indians pushed at her. By the end of the third week she had grown accustomed to the Indian food. Mary's skill at knitting saved her from many hardships. She made a shirt and a cap for King Philip's son, and he invited her to dinner in his wigwam, where she was served a stew made from peas and bear meat. Another Indian gave her a Bible, which she read for comfort during her lonely hours.

But life among the Indians proved hard. Every few days they picked up their camp and moved on, and Mary was loaded down like a pack animal. Sometimes an angry squaw would not feed her or allow her to sleep in a wigwam. Once an Indian tormented her with a story of how her son had been killed and eaten. But unexpectedly, a week later, the boy was brought into camp. Mary embraced him joyously and then combed the lice from his hair.

101

For eleven weeks, as the Indians wandered through northern Massachusetts and southern New Hampshire, Mary Rowlandson clung to her faith that God would somehow save her. She marched under her heavy loads, waded icy rivers, and knitted caps and shirts. Then, in early May, came wonderful news. The Indians had agreed to sell her back to the English for a ransom of twenty pounds sterling. Her son was sold for seven pounds. In late June, Mary learned that her daughter had escaped from the Indians and had found her way to Providence, Rhode Island. Soon the family was reunited.

Not all who were captured by the Indians were as fortunate as Mary Rowlandson and her children. Many died. Others simply disappeared into the forest and were never heard from again.

KING PHILIP IS KILLED

Disaster also awaited King Philip. By the spring of 1676, the English had made an alliance with friendly tribes of Naticks and Niantics. In August an Indian traitor guided the English to King Philip's hiding place in a swamp, and the next morning the chief was killed. His head was cut off and sent to Plymouth, where for twenty-five years it could be seen stuck on a pole—a reminder of terror in the wilderness.

King Philip

Bacon's Rebellion

The small planters of Virginia fight both the Indians and the forces of their tyrannical governor.

During the years of King Philip's War in New England, a different kind of war was going on in Virginia. Called Bacon's Rebellion, it is sometimes described as a dress rehearsal for the American Revolution that would come a hundred years later.

Sir William Berkeley, who was then governor of Virginia, seemed to take no notice of the fact that times were hard. The price of tobacco was falling off and taxes were rising. Many poor people who had sold their services for a period of four or more years to pay for their passage to America had now worked out their terms as "indentured servants." Most of these newly freed servants pushed deeper into the wilderness, cleared their own land, and became small planters in the uplands of Virginia. They did not rely on slaves, as the older plantation owners did, but beat back the forests themselves, with the help of their wives and children. Then, in the summer of 1675, a band of Susquehanna Indians, driven south by the Senecas, began stealing livestock along the Virginia frontier. Shootings and Indian raids followed, and the small planters appealed to the governor for soldiers to protect their lives and their property.

Sir William refused to send the militia. The small planters believed it was because he did not want to upset the very profitable fur trade he was carrying on with the Indians. The planters prepared to raise their own army to put down the Indians on the one hand and defy the governor on the other. All they needed was the right leader.

Great trees were felled as the Virginia settlers cleared the land to build homes and farms.

The man they chose was Nathaniel Bacon, Jr., a fact rather surprising in itself. Bacon was as "well-born" as old Sir William. He had been educated in England before coming to Virginia to build a fine plantation on the banks of the James River. But Bacon was hotheaded, impatient, highly excitable, and he did not like the governor. Moreover, an overseer on Bacon's plantation had been murdered by an Indian, and Bacon wanted revenge. When the upland settlers offered him an army of 300 to command, he gladly accepted.

The war that followed was a strange affair. Bacon and his patchwork army set off to fight the Indians only to learn that the governor had declared him a rebel, had ordered his army disbanded, and had even

In 1676, Nathaniel Bacon and his army of small planters burned the settlement at Jamestown.

Sir William refused to accept defeat. In late summer, Bacon marched his army toward the falls of the James River to fight the Indians. Sir William, defying the House of Burgesses, raised his own army and once more declared Bacon in rebellion. Bacon marched to Middle Plantation (later named Williamsburg) and declared Sir William and his council members traitors to the colony.

Bacon sent one of the colony's armed vessels to capture the governor, but failed through no fault of his own. His soldiers, it was recorded, had been drinking too much of "the juice of the grape." Bacon then turned to fighting his *other* foe, and this time he was successful, driving the Indians from their refuge in the marshes along the shores of the York River.

THE BATTLE FOR JAMESTOWN

Meanwhile, Sir William sailed to Jamestown with an army of 600 men. Bacon was willing to meet the old governor more than halfway and marched his own band back to Jamestown. Bacon's rebels arrived, dead tired, and spent the night throwing up defenses "by the help of the moon light." There was a brisk little skirmish at daybreak, but Sir William refused to fire his cannon. He would not be the first to spill blood, he said.

Bacon acted boldly, seizing "the wives and female relations" of the "gentlemen" in the governor's service and placing them before his defenses "in the face of the enemy." Now Sir William did not dare to order a shot fired. So he did the only thing he could —he left town in a hurry.

Next morning the rebels entered Jamestown, and, because it had been a refuge for the governor, Bacon decided to "lay it level

sent a small force to fight him. Happily, the two armies failed to meet. Bacon stormed into Jamestown, where he was welcomed as a hero. To Sir William's dismay, Bacon was elected to the House of Burgesses, as the Virginia legislative assembly was called. The assembly, taking matters into its own hands, declared war on the Indians and placed Bacon in command of its army.

with the ground." That night the church and the statehouse were burned, along with all the frame houses.

BACON DIES AND SIR WILLIAM IS RESTORED TO POWER

Taking over Sir William's home and orchards at nearby Green Spring, Bacon planned many reforms in the government of Virginia. But he soon died of a fever, and his friends buried him in a secret place. Sir William, restored to power by the king, struck back at his old enemies and hanged twenty-three of those who had taken part in the uprising.

By 1685 the statehouse at Jamestown had been rebuilt, and some people may have wondered if Bacon's Rebellion had accomplished anything. The small planters of Virginia thought it had. They had proved that as Englishmen they were entitled to equal protection under the law. And they had shown the ruling class that if it ruled without justice it might some day lose its power.

THE DEERFIELD MASSACRE

Hoping to drive the English out of western Massachusetts the French and Indians attack Deerfield.

In 1702, Queen Anne of England began a long and bitter struggle with King Louis XIV of France for the control of Europe. Drums beat as the armies of England and France marched to battle, and soon other drums—Indian drums—were beating in the wilderness of Canada.

By May of 1703, Lord Cornbury, Royal Governor of New York, was receiving reports from his spies among the Mohawk Indians. He learned that the French in Canada were stirring up Indian allies to attack the British frontier settlements of New England. Deerfield, the western outpost of Massachusetts, would be a natural target.

Lord Cornbury warned Governor Dudley of Massachusetts of the coming raid, and

Late on a February night, French and Indians swarmed down on Deerfield.

Deerfield prepared to defend itself. The fortifications of the town were strengthened. Children under the age of twelve were kept indoors—a hardship during the summer months when their help was needed in farming. Guards watched the edge of of the wilderness which stretched for 300 miles between Deerfield and Canada. How near were the French and their Indian allies? When would they strike?

The weeks of summer dragged slowly on. Autumn spread flames of gold and scarlet across the forests. The leaves of the trees turned brown and fluttered to the ground—and still there was no attack.

THE ATTACK COMES

The snow came early that year, piling up deep drifts in the forest. As long as the heavy snow lasted, everyone believed the town was safe. Why, an attacking party would freeze to death trying to cross 300 miles of wilderness in this weather!

Late at night, on the last day of February, 1704, the town watchman was leaning against a house. He could hear a mother singing a lullaby to her sick baby. Perhaps the soft, sweet song put him to sleep, or perhaps he was numbed by the cold. In either case, the watchman never gave an alarm. All at once the French and Indians were there. The snowdrifts piled against the walls of the town made it easy for them to climb over the fortifications.

There were more than 250 of them, and they scattered quickly through the town. In the flickering light of torches they broke down doors. Guns blazed and knives flashed. Clubs crashed down on the heads of children and houses were set on fire.

Some of Deerfield's people fought back furiously. Some pleaded for mercy and, if they were lucky, were carried off to captivity in Canada. Some hid in dark corners and, if they were lucky, escaped death or capture. Some simply stood, wide-eyed with fear, as Indians carried firebrands through the houses, ate any food they could find, and picked up any articles of clothing or furniture that took their fancy.

An exceptional case was Mrs. Ruth Catlin, who watched a wounded Frenchman carried into her house and laid upon the floor. The man groaned with pain and called for a drink of water.

Mrs. Catlin said, "I will give you a drink." Her shocked neighbors cried: "How can you do that for your enemy?"

"If thine enemy hunger, feed him," Mrs. Catlin replied quietly. "If he thirst, give him water to drink."

The raiders did not forget Mrs. Catlin's kindness. No harm came to her, and her house was not burned.

When the attack started, there had been 291 persons, ranging in age from eighty-four-year-old Widow Allison to four-week-old John French asleep in their beds. Now 165 had been killed, or captured and forced to march through the cruel wintry weather to Canada.

Many who plunged through the tangled thickets and snow-clogged forests were children. They waded knee deep through rushing woodland streams or forced their way across frozen lakes in the face of fierce north winds. At night they dug away snowdrifts to make a place for their camps. At dawn— they marched on. Whirling snow blinded their eyes, pitiless rains soaked their skins— but on they went, determined to live.

The Deerfield Massacre was the beginning of a desperate struggle for America that would last, off and on, for fifty years. When the Eighteenth Century began—four years before the Deerfield Massacre—the population of colonial America had been estimated at 262,000. Along the Atlantic seacoast, British America stretched from Canada to the border of Spanish-held Florida. In spite of the danger of attack, the colonies continued to grow.

THREE WAYS OF LIFE

*The colonists learn to adapt themselves
to the different conditions of
New England, the Middle Colonies,
and the South.*

By the year 1700, a traveler from Massachusetts to Virginia could not mistake the fact that British America had three ways of life. They changed sharply as the traveler journeyed through hilly, rock-strewn New England, into the "bread colonies" between the fertile valleys of the Hudson and Potomac Rivers, and on to the plantations of the South.

Anyone who made such a journey in those days needed to be brave. Narrow, dusty roads wound through dank swamps and dark forests. There were few bridges over the creeks and rivers, so that the traveler was often forced to wade the cold, swift streams.

At nightfall, when the traveler stopped at a village inn, the best he could expect was a poor place to rest his tired bones. Sarah Kemble Knight, a Boston schoolteacher who journeyed to New York by horseback in 1704, described a typical room she was offered as "a little lean-to chamber, furnished among other rubbish with a high bed and a low one, a long table, a low bench, and a bottomless chair."

Like many travelers of the time, Mrs. Knight chose to go to bed supperless: "The landlady came in, with her hair about her ears, and hands at full play scratching. She told us she had some mutton which she would broil, which I was glad to hear. But I suppose she forgot to wash her scratchers. In a little time she brought it in. . . . My guide said it smelt strong of head sauce. We left it, and paid six pence a piece for our dinner, which was only smell."

In New England, the traveler soon realized that this was no region for profitable

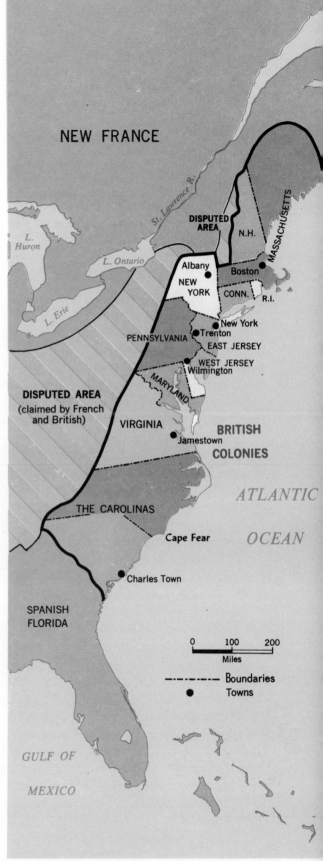

Colonies in the eastern part of North America in 1700.

The colonists lived mostly by trading and farming.

farming. Much of New England was covered with mountains, and elsewhere the rocky soil made plowing and cultivating crops difficult. Winters were long and hard and summers short. With the exception of the Connecticut, New England rivers could not be traveled by boat for any great distance, so that transportation from farm to market presented a special problem. As a result, New Englanders became merchants, manufacturers, shipowners, shipbuilders, and bankers. New England became a center of trade and shipbuilding. Ships from Newburyport, Ipswich, Gloucester, Salem, Boston, New Bedford, Newport, Providence, New London, and New Haven sailed proudly over the oceans of the world.

As soon as a traveler entered the Middle Colonies, he was in a different world. The fertile valleys of the Hudson and Mohawk Rivers in New York were a farmer's paradise. So were the wide, gently sloping river valleys of New Jersey and Pennsylvania, where wheat took the place of corn as the chief crop. Here the fields also yielded fine harvests of rye, oats, barley, hay, vegetables, and fruits. Markets were close at hand and easy to reach. With fast-growing cities like New York and Philadelphia, the Middle Colonies gave promise of one day equaling New England as a center of trade.

Entering the South the traveler saw still a different way of life. Here was a country that lived by one product—tobacco, rice, or indigo. Often, in hopes of gaining a quick profit, the Southern planter raised one cash crop and had to rely on other colonies for his food. Often, too, he failed to fertilize worn-out fields. Land was cheap; he simply cleared new acres.

Slaves gave the Southern planter inexpensive labor, and many plantations grew into little kingdoms. He looked on his slave —even when he treated him kindly—the same way he looked on his horse or his plow. They were all "property." There were also slaves in the Middle Colonies and New England, but they were fewer in number and played a less important part.

Clearly, British America was growing without a single plan or pattern. The three regions were going their own individual ways, like so many different little nations. Except for the hardy traveler on foot or horseback, or the sailor touching at the coastal ports of Boston, New York, Philadelphia, and Charleston, there was very little communication between colonies.

Yet change was coming more quickly than anyone expected. On Milk Street in Boston on January 6, 1706, a maker of soap and candles listened to the lusty howls of a newborn son, his fifteenth child. That red-faced infant would go down in history as "the first civilized American" and "the apostle of modern times."

When he was ten years old, Ben Franklin dreamed of going to sea.

Benjamin Franklin

*Franklin sets himself up as a
printer in Philadelphia.*

Young Benjamin Franklin lived happily
with his big family on Milk Street.

"I do not remember when I could not
read," Ben recalled in later years. At the age
of eight he was sent to a grammar school
with the intention of preparing him for the
ministry. His father, Josiah Franklin, soon
realized that with his large family he could
not afford to give Ben the years of long edu-
cation this calling required. Ben was placed
with George Brownell, a private teacher.
"Under him," Ben said, "I acquired fair
writing pretty soon, but I failed in the
arithmetic, and made no progress."

At the age of ten, Ben began helping his
father in the business of a tallow chandler
and soap boiler. He cut wicks for candles,
filled the dripping molds, attended the
shop, and ran errands. Ben did not like the
trade and wanted to go to sea.

Josiah Franklin would not hear of it, yet
he was a good father. For hours man and
boy walked the streets of Boston, watching
all sorts of craftsmen at work in the hope
that the lad could find "some trade or other
on land" that he liked.

Always a bookish fellow, Ben was happy
when his half brother James returned from
England in 1717 with a printing press and
type to set up a business in Boston. He was
now eleven years old, and he signed papers,
agreeing to serve as an apprentice until he
reached twenty-one.

111

Ben fancied himself a poet in those years, and composed and printed two long ballads that he offered for sale. One ballad, *The Lighthouse Tragedy*, telling of the drowning of a captain and his two daughters, was a popular success. Ben was quite proud of himself until his father spoke his mind. A poet? Who could afford a poet in the Franklin family?

Sometimes it was difficult to guess what Ben would do next. He read a book that convinced him he should give up eating meat and live on vegetables—and he persuaded James to give him the board money that was saved on his cheaper diet. This he spent on books.

FRANKLIN LEAVES BOSTON

In 1721, James began to publish a newspaper, the *New England Courant*. Soon a series of articles, signed by "Silence Dogood," was slipped under the door of his office. James liked and published them until he discovered that the author was Ben. These two were quick to quarrel, for James thought of himself more as Ben's master than as his brother.

James never hesitated to criticize civic and religious leaders in his newspaper, and he soon found himself in jail. Ben now forgot the quarrels and carried on the publication of the *Courant*. He was having a wonderful time: "I made bold to give our rulers some rubs in it, which my brother took very kindly, while others began to consider me in an unfavorable light, as a young genius that had a turn for libelling."

Once James was released from prison, he and Ben quickly began quarreling again. "Perhaps I was too saucy and provoking," Ben admitted in later years. All the same, he decided to strike off on his own.

When Deborah Read first saw Franklin eating a roll as he walked down the street, she thought him ridiculous. Later, however, she married him.

A three-day voyage brought him to New York. Finding no work there, he pushed on to Philadelphia. The trip across lower New York Bay to Amboy, New Jersey, was long and stormy, and Ben rescued "a drunken Dutchman" who fell overboard by pulling him up by his hair. In three days of weary walking Ben covered the fifty miles across New Jersey to the Delaware River. Hungry, tired, and almost penniless, he reached Philadelphia next morning. It was a day he never forgot:

"I walked up the street, gazing about till near the market-house I met a boy with bread. I had made many a meal on bread, and, inquiring where he got it, I went immediately to the baker's. . . . Not considering or knowing the difference of money, nor the greater cheapness nor the names of his bread, I bade him give three-penny worth of any sort. He gave me, accordingly, three great puffy rolls. I was surprised at the quantity, but took it, and, having no room in my pockets, walked off with a roll under each arm, and eating the other. Thus I went up Market Street as far as Fourth Street, passing by the door of Mr. Read, my future wife's father; when she, standing at the door, saw me, and thought I made . . . a most awkward, ridiculous appearance. . . ."

Ben gave his other two rolls to a mother and her child. Then he attended a Quaker meeting. He fell sound asleep, but the friendly Quakers did not awaken him until the meeting ended.

FRANKLIN FINDS WORK

Ben soon found employment in the printing shop of Samuel Keimer. He roomed at the Reads'—where Miss Deborah decided he was neither awkward nor ridiculous. Such was the nature of this remarkable young fellow that in a very short time he counted among his friends Sir William Keith, the Provincial Governor.

LIVELY TIMES IN CHARLESTON

Pirates terrorize the seas, but most are caught and hanged.

In the year 1717, James Logan, Secretary of Pennsylvania, reported that 1,500 pirates were sweeping the seas from Newfoundland to Brazil. Driven by the English fleet from their main hide-out in the Bahamas, the pirates made their final stand along the coast of the Carolinas.

One of them was the bloodthirsty Robert Thatch (or Teach), better known as "Blackbeard." In June of 1718 he appeared before Charleston harbor with a forty-gun frigate accompanied by three sloops. His crews numbered about 400 men. He quickly captured several vessels, including one that carried many prominent Charleston citizens.

Blackbeard chuckled at his good luck. He made out a long list of medicines and other supplies he needed and sent a party to Charleston with a message for the governor. Unless he received these supplies within forty-eight hours he would send the governor the heads of all the Charlestonians he held as prisoners. Charleston had no defense against Blackbeard's frigate. He was given his supplies and the prisoners were released. They arrived home almost naked, for the pirates had even robbed them of their clothes. Blackbeard sailed back to Pamlico Sound, still chuckling.

BONNET THREATENS CHARLESTON

Soon after this, another pirate threatened Charleston—Stede Bonnet. Stede offered the strangest excuse in history for taking up piracy. He said it was the only way he could find to escape from a quarrelsome wife.

The colonists feared the pirates, who looted any vessel they could catch.

Bold when attacking the helpless, Stede Bonnet turned coward when facing the gallows.

Stede's dreadful deeds were known—and feared—all the way from Barbados to the coast of Maine. It was no wonder that Charlestonians were worried when, late in the summer of 1718, they heard that Stede Bonnet, aboard his ship the *Revenge,* stood off their harbor.

BONNET IS CAPTURED

Robert Johnson, the Governor of South Carolina, decided that he had had enough pirates. He sent two armed ships under the command of William Rhett to deal with Stede. A merry chase followed, ending at the entrance to the Cape Fear River. Here Stede's ships and Rhett's grounded on sand bars.

The battle now depended on which side the rising tide favored. If Stede's ship broke free first, clearly he would have the colonists at his mercy. Life or death for Charleston depended on every ripple as the tide came in. All at once one of Rhett's ships floated free, coming around and making for Stede's still grounded vessel. The pirates were forced to surrender.

In defeat, Stede was no hero. He whined and begged for his life, trying to invent excuses for the terrible things he had done. Charleston's citizens marched him to Execution Dock and watched as he and his crew were hung in chains.

The flood tide of piracy was running out in North America. A few weeks after Stede and his rascals swung from the gallows, two stout cruisers from Virginia found Blackbeard and his men lurking in Ocracoke Inlet on the North Carolina coast. A bloody battle was fought and Blackbeard was killed. The colonists hung the survivors of the crew, and the lead ship returned up the James River with the severed head of Blackbeard decorating her bowsprit.

115

THE "MISSISSIPPI BUBBLE"

*Hundreds of Frenchmen invest
their savings in the New World,
only to lose them.*

From the beginning of the Eighteenth Century, France had acted on the belief that the English intended to seize possession of the mouth of the Mississippi River. In 1702, a new and stronger settlement was established at Mobile, replacing Biloxi as the capital of the Louisiana province.

Two years later the excited people of Mobile witnessed the arrival of the *Pelican.* Aboard this snug little vessel were twenty-three young girls who had been brought as wives and home builders for French settlers in the Louisiana wilderness. Each girl was provided with a *cassette,* or trunk, and an outfit of clothing. Within a month twenty-two of the "cassette girls" had found husbands, and the one still unmarried was described as "hard to please." Before the year ended, the first white child was born in the province.

FRANCE BUILDS TRADING POSTS

The French pushed steadily ahead to secure control of the great valley that was the life line of mid-America. Bienville, the new governor of Louisiana, and Cadillac, the founder of Detroit, worked together in exploring the lower Mississippi and Red Rivers. French trading posts began to dot the wilderness far up the Missouri River and along the lower Ohio Valley.

In May, 1713, a French frigate brought another shipment of girls in search of husbands—twenty-five this time. Twenty-three more came in 1718, another eighty in 1719, a like number in 1721. Each girl was carefully selected by officers of the church, and nuns watched over them until they had made a good "match."

Another proof that the French were in earnest about developing the Mississippi Valley was the king's selection in 1712 of Antoine Crozat to manage this territory. Crozat was one of the great merchants and bankers of France, and in his hands was placed all the trade of Louisiana.

Crozat had his troubles. The Spanish barred his ships from their ports. The English were unfriendly and looked the other way as pirates took their toll of French ships. By 1717, Crozat was more than willing to give up his dream of making a fortune in gold, silver, mineral ores, furs, and trade with the Indians. Heavily in debt, he surrendered his charter.

A remarkable fellow—some called him a scoundrel—now stepped forward to take over Crozat's unfinished work in Louisiana. His name was John Law. A tricky Scot, Law was a magician at juggling money—usually

other people's money. He had risen to high favor with Louis XIV of France.

In 1718—the year New Orleans was founded and France could believe that she had at last secured control of the Mississippi—Law launched his campaign to interest investors in his new company. He spoke of the great riches in gold and silver Louisiana possessed. He told how hundreds of settlers wanted to rush to Louisiana and of the profits his company was certain to earn.

Thousands of Frenchmen believed him. Scrub women, maids, small merchants, and farmers, bank clerks and shopkeepers scraped and saved to buy stock in Law's wilderness empire. The rich also invested heavily and pawned their jewels to buy more stock. All over Paris, the same talk was heard. Everyone would soon be rich.

Then, in 1720, the truth came out. There was no gold or silver, no rush of settlers. So,

all at once, the great "Mississippi Bubble" exploded. Hundreds of investors were ruined. And Law, whose bag had long been packed, was already hurrying out of France.

Yet Law's talents for advertising had not been entirely wasted. The legend he had created of the wealth to be gained in Louisiana lingered on, and slowly the population of the region increased. French adventurers continued to push up the Arkansas River (where Arkansas Post had been established), into Illinois country (with settlements at Cahokia and Kaskaskia), and up the Wabash into Indiana (where they built Vincennes). By 1739 they had founded Ste. Geneviève in Missouri. Along the lower Mississippi, French plantations pushed out to the river front, growing tobacco at first, then rice, indigo, and some cotton. By 1751 the planters had introduced sugar as a crop of the Deep South.

In 1704, twenty-three young women arrived in Mobile to become brides of the French settlers.

Spanish settlers held a fair at Taos every spring.

"RANCHEROS" OF THE OLD SOUTHWEST

The Spanish build missions and establish ranches on the plains of New Mexico and Texas.

The Spanish were strengthening their hold on Texas and New Mexico. A mission was built at San Antonio, Texas, in 1718. In the years that followed, the energetic friars, supported by military forces, established ten more missions and four new towns in Texas.

But the real empire builders in this region were the large landholders, or *rancheros*. Their great cattle ranches and comfortable homes, or *haciendas,* began to spread across this fine range country. The land changed under their control as great ditches were dug to irrigate food and cotton crops. Horsemen rode the ranges and looked after great herds of cattle and sheep.

Indian labor was used to produce woven cloth and articles of silver and turquoise in the settlements of Santa Fe and Albuquerque. Spanish traders went northward—up the Colorado and the Arkansas Rivers and into the desert of the Great Salt Lake. Each year the fair at Taos was a time for song, dancing, and hard drinking. Santa Fe was becoming well known to men seeking quick profits — respectable trappers, *rancheros,* merchants, smugglers, horse thieves.

In the struggle for North America, the French were gaining in the lower Mississippi, the Spanish in Florida, Texas, and New Mexico. Meanwhile, many thousands of miles from the New World, another chapter was opening in the developing story of America.

Toward the Arctic Sun

Russian explorers sail east through stormy seas and fog to the northwest coast of the New World.

Peter the Great, Czar of All the Russias, was a man of deep intelligence. He welcomed scholars from France and Germany to his court at St. Petersburg, where they helped to establish the Russian Academy of Science.

Strange reports had been reaching St. Petersburg from across the Ural Mountains. After heavy storms along Russia's Pacific coast line, waves washed up timber unlike the wood of native trees. Often the waves also left on the shores the bodies of strange animals with spears in them. Could this mean that there was inhabited land nearby to the east—land that perhaps joined the continents of Asia and North America? The scholars urged the czar to solve this mystery, and in 1725 he sent an expedition to see whether land linked Russia with America.

To lead this expedition, Peter the Great called to St. Petersburg a Danish-born navigator named Vitus Jonassen Bering. Now forty-four years of age, Bering had spent half his life on the seas in the service of the British East India Company and the Russian navy. Though stubborn and hot-tempered, he was a capable leader. He and his party traveled for months, at times trapped by howling blizzards. They trudged across hundreds of miles of Arctic land until they reached the coast of the stormy North Pacific. Here they built a ship, the *Gabriel,* and in July, 1727, set off to find a link between the continents. St. Petersburg was 5,000 miles behind them.

For a month, as the *Gabriel* plunged through rolling seas, the days were all alike —a dreary succession of calm and fog, wind and rain. In early August some Siberian

Bering and his party made their way across Siberia, then built a boat and set sail.

119

Russian explorers were the first Europeans to see the Aleutians and Alaska.

Chuckchees appeared, paddling their skin boats, but they could not be talked into coming aboard the *Gabriel*. Two days later Bering and his crew sighted and named St. Lawrence Island. Bucking strong head winds, they passed through the waters now known as the Bering Strait. At one time Bering was at a point where only fifty-four miles separated East Cape, Siberia, from Prince of Wales, Alaska, but fog prevented him from discovering that fact. He decided that an arm of the Pacific Ocean must divide Asia and America, and at last turned back toward Russia.

BERING'S SECOND TRIP

More than five years had passed when Bering returned to St. Petersburg, and Peter the Great was dead. No one was satisfied with Bering's report, and the Empress declared that Bering must again search for the possible land link. He was also to "explore the North American coast as far south as the Spanish possessions in Mexico." It was June of 1741 before Bering was again ready to sail the icy North Pacific in another vessel, the *St. Peter*. At noon on July 16, Bering and his men sighted the mainland of Alaska. Before them rose a majestic mountain that they named Mount St. Elias. Four days later they discovered Kayak Island and a party was sent ashore in two longboats.

Kayak Island held many fascinations for the Russian explorers. Among the plants they saw was Alaska's state flower, the forget-me-not. The people had vanished from the huts of logs and rough planks that they had roofed with bark and dried grass. Inside the dwellings were copper pots and plates, a whetstone, a rattle made of clay, some broken arrows, bits of dried fish, and a strand of rope made of seaweed. Behind

They were astonished to find traces of an abandoned village on Kayak Island.

them was a mountain covered with a thick forest. The Russians could find no trace of a road. Bering seemed to feel this deserted place was evil and sailed away as soon as he could.

BERING DIES

Beating a course to the south-southwest through fog, rain, drenching gales, and pounding waves, the *St. Peter* pushed homeward. Sailors began to come down with scurvy, and in September Bering fell ill. It was a miserable voyage. By November the steersman was so weak that two men had to hold him up as he stood at the helm. Not until December did the *St. Peter* reach the Commander Islands. There Bering died. He was buried on a sandy hillside with a plain Greek cross marking his grave. Of the seventy-seven men who had sailed with Bering, thirty-one had died by mid-

January. But Bering's crew brought back proof that there was a plentiful supply of fur-bearing animals, such as the sea otter, in the region they had visited. And there was money to be made in the fur trade, if a man was willing to take the risks.

THE RUSSIAN FUR TRADERS

In 1745, Michael Novidiskov became the first white man to sail to Attu, the extreme western islet of the Aleutian chain. Soon others followed. They were cruel conquerors, these Russian traders, and it is claimed that many Aleuts committed suicide rather than suffer under the Russians. But the rulers in St. Petersburg were interested in their ten per cent of the profits from each voyage. They had no feeling for the welfare of the people who lived in that far-off country they called "great land" or "mainland" —in Aleut, *Al-ay-ek-sa.*

121

POOR RICHARD IN PHILADELPHIA

Franklin turns his restless mind to many projects, the most popular of which is Poor Richard's Almanack.

While the Russians were busy attempting to gain a hold on the far northern regions of the continent, life was changing in the colonies along the Atlantic seaboard. America's first theater was built in Williamsburg, Virginia, in 1716. Five years later Gustavus Hesselius, a Swedish immigrant to Delaware, received the first public grant as an artist when he was commissioned to paint "The Last Supper" for the Church of St. Barnabas in Queen Anne Parish, Maryland.

In 1731, John Bartram established America's first botanical gardens near Philadelphia, and that same year America's first public concert was given "at Mr. Pelham's great room" in Boston. An almshouse (poorhouse) supported by public funds, probably the first of its kind, was established in Philadelphia in 1732, and two years later William Bull of South Carolina became the first American to receive a medical degree. A performance of *Flora, or Hob in the Well* brought the opera to Charleston — and America — in 1735, and in 1737 New York's Trinity Church got the colonies' first organ.

These were also years when that remarkable young man, Benjamin Franklin, began to make his influence felt in Philadelphia. By 1729, Ben had prospered to the point where he had become owner and publisher of the *Pennsylvania Gazette*. Two years later he established the first circulating library in America. No one knew quite what to expect next from Ben's restless mind. He flew a kite in a rainstorm to prove that lightning was a form of electricity. His long list of inventions included the lightning rod, a stove, bifocal glasses, and a rocking

Benjamin Franklin

chair. He organized the first fire department in Philadelphia, helped to organize the first hospital in America, reformed the city's police system, and founded the school that became the University of Pennsylvania.

From 1732 to 1757, however, Franklin's greatest gift to colonial America was the publication of *Poor Richard's Almanack*. Aside from the Bible, no publication was more popular in the average home. Ben had a way of belonging to Americans. He understood why they believed and acted the way they did. The sayings that he composed for *Poor Richard* were more than catchy phrases, easy to remember.

When Ben wrote, "A penny saved is a penny earned," or "Little strokes fell great oaks," he was speaking of the qualities of thrift and industry a person needed to get ahead in the colonies. When Ben wrote, "Like cats in airpumps, to subsist [exist] we strive," his fellow Americans, beating back a wilderness, chuckled at this image of themselves. Some 10,000 copies of *Poor Richard's Almanack* were sold each year. Colonial America liked Ben's homely advice, agreeing with him that "God helps them that help themselves."

A BLOW FOR FREEDOM

John Peter Zenger, a New York printer, fights for a free press in America.

The growth of newspapers in the colonies was another sign that America was shaping a new life in the New World. Philadelphia's first newspaper, the *American Weekly Mercury*, began publication in 1719. New York followed with the *Gazette* in 1725, as did Maryland, with the *Maryland Gazette* of Annapolis in 1727. The *South Carolina Gazette* at Charleston and the *Rhode Island Gazette* at Newport began publication in 1732.

The trial of John Peter Zenger in 1735 was a milestone in American history.

John Peter Zenger, a poor German printer whose little shop in New York City barely provided for his family, struck the blow that changed newspapers in America. Like many New Yorkers, Zenger watched with displeasure the highhanded actions of William Cosby, who became the royal governor in 1732. Cosby would give no grants of land to settlers unless he was guaranteed a personal profit. He dealt harshly with the Quakers. In order to rule as he pleased, he dismissed the chief justice of the colony's supreme court. Since the publisher of the *Gazette* was also the public printer, no criticism of Cosby was permitted in the columns of the city's only newspaper.

THE NEW YORK "WEEKLY JOURNAL"

Infuriated citizens appealed to Zenger. Would he publish a rival newspaper if they provided the money? Zenger pointed out that he needed more than money. He was poor in English spelling and grammar. No matter, replied his friends. The articles would be written for him. Under these cir-

cumstances the New York *Weekly Journal* appeared. Article after article pictured Cosby and his court party as scamps. New Yorkers read the *Journal* with eyes popping and tongues wagging. Often Zenger had to print extra editions to meet the demand.

Cosby struck back by charging Zenger with "seditious libels" (accusations), which tended to fill the minds of the people with "contempt of His Majesty's government." Zenger was thrown into jail and the bail was set so high that he had no hope of gaining his release. The two attorneys who offered to defend Zenger were disbarred so that they could not handle the case. A young lawyer, clearly no match for Cosby's attorney general, was appointed by the court.

The greatest lawyer in the colonies in those days was Andrew Hamilton of Philadelphia. Troubled with gout, Hamilton described himself as "old and weak." The trip from Philadelphia to New York was long and difficult, and no one could have blamed Hamilton if he had begged off defending Zenger. But this grand old man put the principle involved in this case before his

124

Andrew Hamilton's oratory freed Zenger, and also won freedom for the press.

personal comfort. Unless the people had a right to complain against "the arbitrary attempts of men in power," what justice did life offer them?

ZENGER STANDS TRIAL

John Peter Zenger stood trial on August 4, 1735. Stirred by the case, people crowded into the little courtroom. Then came the dramatic moment—the door opened and famous old Andrew Hamilton hobbled on his gout-stricken feet into the room. All at once the members of Cosby's official party looked uneasy. With dark glances they followed Hamilton as he slowly lumbered to his seat.

The attorney general presented the charge to the jury—the articles Zenger had published were "false, scandalous, malicious, and seditious." Old Hamilton thundered back that he knew perfectly well Zenger's articles were "libelous." Could the attorney general prove they were "false?" But the governor's party stood by the accepted law of England at the time: Truth was no defense. Persons who made state-ments that tended "to disquiet the minds of the people" must be punished.

Such law, Hamilton knew, was the weapon of tyrants. The only way he could save Zenger—and freedom of the press in America—was to convince the jury of this. He spoke brilliantly. If men were denied the right to write and speak their minds about the conduct of men in power, what then? "The next step may make them slaves," said Hamilton. He also said: "The loss of liberty to a generous mind is worse than death. . . . The man who loves his country prefers its liberty to all other considerations, well knowing that without liberty life is a misery."

The jury was out but a few minutes. It gave its verdict: "Not guilty!" Cheers burst from the crowd. Old Andrew Hamilton bowed, having won a victory that would make him remembered forever by freedom-loving men. That night he was given a celebration at the Black Horse Tavern, and next morning, when he started home to Philadelphia, boats in the harbor fired salutes in his honor.

A COLONY OF DEBTORS

James Oglethorpe settles Georgia with prisoners whose only crime was their inability to pay their debts.

Another man who struck a blow against injustice was James Oglethorpe. During the Eighteenth Century, anyone in Great Britain who failed to pay money he owed could be thrown into jail. An architect named Robert Castell, imprisoned for this reason, contracted smallpox and died. Castell had been a close friend of James Oglethorpe, who, as a member of Parliament, now made an investigation of English debtors' prisons. His findings were a scandal. Jailers and their deputies, he reported, treated prisoners brutally, made them pay enormous prices for small comforts, and were guilty of many other crimes. Oglethorpe could not forget the misery of these prisoners. They deserved a new life, a better life—and thus he came to the idea of planting the colony of Georgia in the New World.

Hardheaded, practical considerations led the British government to listen to Oglethorpe's plan of bringing debtors to America. There they could "not only gain a comfortable subsistence for themselves and families, but also strengthen our colonies and increase the trade, navigation, and wealth of these our realms." What the king wanted more than anything else was a new buffer land between his now prosperous colony of South Carolina and Spanish and French troublemakers to the south and west. So Georgia was created as a colony that would extend from the Atlantic to the Pacific Oceans, with the Savannah and Altamaha Rivers as its northern and southern boundaries. The king did not worry over the fact that he was claiming parts of Florida, Louisiana, and Texas, and including Albuquerque, Socorro, and other New Mexico settlements in Georgia's territory.

Oglethorpe sailed for America in November, 1732, with 116 settlers. After seven stormy weeks at sea, the voyagers reached Charleston. Oglethorpe plunged at once into building his new state in the wilderness. He was a natural leader and a man who was friendly to everyone. Quickly the Indians came to trust and love him. He welcomed to Georgia people of many religious faiths—Protestants from France, Jews from Germany and Portugal, Lutherans and Moravians from the Rhineland districts, Presbyterians from the Scottish Highlands. Georgia also became a colony where Negro slavery was prohibited.

An article in the Charleston *Gazette* described the kind of leader Oglethorpe was: "He's extremely well beloved by all his people. The general title they give him is *father*. If any of them is sick, he immediately visits them. If any difference arises, he's the person that decides it." Before Oglethorpe returned to England in March, 1734, he had established eleven communities among the forests on the banks of the Savannah River. The largest town was Savannah, with neat gardens, wide streets, and ample provision for houses, churches, and water supply.

Among those who accompanied Oglethorpe when he returned to England were Tomochichi, ninety-year-old chief of the Yamacraw Indians, his wife, his grandnephew, and five braves. Londoners treated the Indians as though they were visiting royalty. They were welcomed with the ringing of bells. They were taken to fairs, to shops, to the theater, and reviews of troops were staged in their honor. The royal household greeted them, for Tomochichi was a dignified old man who changed many British ideas about the so-called savages of America. When it came time for Tomochichi and his party to return home, the chief could not hide his grief at leaving Ogle-

Tomochichi, chief of a branch of the Creek tribe, was welcomed with parades, fairs, and banquets when Oglethorpe took him over to London.

thorpe. The occasion, the old Indian said, "was like the day of death."

Oglethorpe knew how to win new friends and support for his colony. Among the gifts he had brought from America were thirty pounds of raw Georgia-grown silk that he had woven into a dress for the queen, which won her affection for both Oglethorpe and his colony. The king was more interested in a plan to build a chain of twenty forts as a safeguard against the Spanish and French. After a year and a half in England, Oglethorpe was anxious to return to his beloved Georgia.

THE SPANIARDS THREATEN GEORGIA

Troubled years were ahead. The Spaniards at St. Augustine did not like the rapid growth of the colony to the north. They liked it even less when they learned how Oglethorpe was beginning to string his forts along the frontier. They heard that Oglethorpe, dressed in a kilt, had sailed up Altamaha Sound to visit the Scottish Highlanders who had settled at New Inverness (now Darien). With bagpipes sounding, the Scotsmen had swarmed down to the beach in

127

Oglethorpe and his Highlanders rushed from ambush and routed the Spanish.

their plaids. The Spaniards suspected that Oglethorpe had come to plan another fort and were not amused.

The Spaniards demanded that the British clear out of all of Georgia and South Carolina below Port Royal. Oglethorpe's reply was to prepare for battle. In July, 1742, a Spanish fleet of thirty-six vessels, bringing a land force of 3,000, entered the harbor at St. Simons. Oglethorpe's army, even including friendly Indians, numbered less than 1,000. "I know the enemy are far more numerous than we," he told his soldiers, "but I rely on the valor of our men, and by God's help, I believe we will be victorious."

OGLETHORPE ATTACKS

Oglethorpe planned a sneak attack at night upon the Spanish encampment at St. Simons. Cautiously he moved along a road that was protected by a dense live oak forest on one side and a deep swamp on the other. Nearing the camp, a Frenchman in Oglethorpe's little army fired his musket and deserted to the enemy.

Oglethorpe decided to fight trickery with trickery. He wrote a letter that made the deserter seem to be a spy planted among the Spaniards. The letter told the "spy" to persuade the Spaniards that the Georgian forces were weak and to attack at once. If the Spaniards would not attack, the letter went on, then the "spy" was to persuade the Spaniards to remain at St. Simons three days longer. By then a British fleet with 2,000 land forces would attack St. Augustine. All this "information," of course, was nonsense and, as Oglethorpe planned, the letter was carried "by accident" to the Spanish commander.

The trick worked and the French deserter was hung as a spy. Then some vessels from Carolina, appearing by luck, were mistaken for the British fleet sailing to St. Augustine. The Spaniards made a hasty attack along the road flanked by live oak forest

and swamp. Oglethorpe and his kilted Highlanders had set a perfect ambush, and almost the whole Spanish attacking force was captured or killed. A second wave of Spaniards, pushing forward to relieve their comrades, also was raked mercilessly by the flaming muskets. In confusion, the invaders fled to their ships.

OGLETHORPE RETURNS TO ENGLAND

Oglethorpe had outgeneraled the Spaniards and had probably saved both Georgia and South Carolina from conquest and ruin. Returning to England in 1743, he lived out his life there; he was almost ninety when he died. He had one deep regret: in later years Negro slavery was permitted in his beloved free colony of Georgia, and by 1760, one third of the inhabitants of the colony of Georgia were slaves.

War Clouds

In Europe, France and England sign a treaty of peace, but remain rivals.

In the ancient European city of Aix-la-Chapelle, a famous treaty was signed in 1748 by officials from Great Britain, France, Holland, Germany, Spain, and Genoa. They hoped the treaty would bring at least a hundred years of peace. Yet the ink of their signatures had scarcely dried before those old foes—France and England—began sowing the seed of future war in their colonies in the New World.

Cornwallis was enraged when the Micmacs refused to obey his orders.

For twenty years the Acadians in Nova Scotia had accepted British rule. Farming people of French descent, they lived for their families and their church. The Acadians asked only that they be free to follow their own religious beliefs and that they never be required to bear arms against fellow Frenchmen or their Indian friends.

But the presence of so many French Roman Catholics in Nova Scotia troubled Governor Shirley of Massachusetts. Stubborn and strong-willed, he wanted direct and brutal action. Uproot the lot of them, Shirley urged, and scatter them among the English colonies where their Catholic ways would be no "menace."

As a substitute for this cruel policy, the authorities in England decided to accomplish the same result by settling large numbers of Protestants among the Acadians. So, in 1749, about 1,400 British soldiers and marines were given land in Nova Scotia and settled in a dreary place they named Halifax.

Colonel Cornwallis, the leader of these British colonists, puffed out his chest, clicked his polished boots, and spoke snappishly. Acadians in Nova Scotia, he said, 131

ours forever, and we will not yield it to any man!"

Turning on his heel, the Micmac stalked off. Cornwallis pushed his chin forward. The Indians of the Nova Scotia peninsula, he growled, were "banditti, ruffians or rebels" who must be hunted down and "taken or killed." He would pay a fat reward for every scalp brought to him.

The actions of Cornwallis showed that Britain had decided to be firm with its colonial subjects. There was too much loose talk in America. There were too many men like John Peter Zenger and the Boston preacher who told his congregation that it was "lawful and glorious" to disobey rulers when they were unjust and unwise. The British were determined to keep such ideas from spreading. And, above all, the British did not intend to be pushed around by their old enemies, the French.

must take an oath of allegiance to Great Britain and must obey the laws like other British subjects. Heartsick, the Acadians begged for the chance to sell their lands and move to a part of Canada where they could live at peace among fellow Frenchmen.

"Take the oath or your property will be confiscated," Cornwallis replied. "It is for me to command: you to obey."

THE MICMACS DEFY ENGLAND

Cornwallis had other problems as well. For some time Jesuit priests in Canada had been stirring up the Indians to a series of raids along the New England frontier, and Cornwallis intended to stop this. A Micmac chief, standing straight and defiant between two young warriors, listened stonily as Cornwallis demanded that the Micmacs give in to British authority.

"The land on which you sleep is ours," the chief said. "We sprang from it as do the trees, and the grass, and the flowers. It is

FRENCH AGENTS CALL ON THE ACADIANS TO REVOLT

But the French had plans of their own. A French force supported by the Micmacs seized the isthmus that connected Nova Scotia to the mainland. French agents mingled with the Acadians, calling on them to give up their allegiance to England. Cornwallis advanced with 400 soldiers to put down this rebellion. He came with too little and he came too late. The bewildered Acadians watched a Jesuit priest setting fire to the church as an example of how they must burn their houses and flee across the river.

Cornwallis was beaten back, but the British had learned a lesson. In June, 1755, British troops advanced once more, this time with enough men to do the job. They caught the French and Indians at Fort Beauséjour and handled them roughly. For those who had dreamed of a century of peace at Aix-la-Chapelle, the awakening had come all too quickly.

THE GATHERING STORM

The British send a scout to explore the Ohio River Valley, but the French are also active there.

Off Cape Sable, an island at the southern tip of Nova Scotia, a British man-of-war captured a number of French vessels. Hope faded for a peaceful settlement between the two old foes. Soon they found something else to quarrel over—the rich and undeveloped Ohio Valley.

The members of the Ohio Land Company had no intention of letting the French take any part of the vast regions claimed by the Virginia colony. Although the land originally granted to Virginia had been whittled away to provide for the colonies of Maryland, the Carolinas, and Pennsylvania, Virginia in 1750 remained an enormous empire stretching into the mists of an unexplored wilderness. Virginia territory included what today is the western part of Pennsylvania and the states of West Virginia, Kentucky, Ohio, Indiana, Illinois, Michigan, and Wisconsin.

Gist traveled alone through mountain snows, and saw lands no white man had seen before.

133

What were the possibilities for trade and settlement in these lands? The Ohio Land Company wanted to know the answer, for it was preparing to push westward. In the autumn of 1750 it hired Christopher Gist, a bold woodsman and friend of the Indians, to cross the mountains and report on the country.

Gist was to report on the best mountain passes, explore the land as far as the falls of the Ohio River (at present-day Louisville), search out valleys that could be cultivated, and learn the strength of various Indian tribes. Meanwhile, the company sent to London for goods suitable for trade with the Indians.

GIST STARTS HIS JOURNEY

Gist plunged into the wilderness. He crossed the Blue Ridge Mountains and the Shenandoah Valley, waded through the snowdrifts in the Alleghenies, and swam the Ohio River. At Logstown the Muskingum Indians received him coldly. "You are come to settle the Indians' land," they said. "You never shall go home safe."

Gist was not easily frightened. He went on to meet the Ottawas, who were friendly with the French, and the Wyandots, who seemed glad to see him. At a Wyandot village he came face to face with George Croghan, whom Pennsylvania had sent into the wilderness to establish trade with the Indians of the Northwest. Croghan and Gist were working for rival groups, but they put aside their differences and continued the journey through the Indian territory together.

Across the Muskingum—the "beautiful river"—they traveled among the Delawares and the Shawnees until they came at last to the wonderful country of the Miamis. This confederacy of Indians was even more powerful than the Iroquois, and the British wanted them for allies. Strings of wampum were exchanged and a treaty of peace

signed. At that moment four Ottawas appeared with presents from the French, and the chief of the Miamis set up the French flag beside the British flag. Then he spoke bitterly to the Ottawas:

"The path of the French is bloody, and was made so by them. We have made a road plain for our brothers, the English, and your fathers have made it foul and crooked, and have made some of our brethren prisoners. This we look upon as an injury done to us."

The chief of the Miamis turned his back on the Ottawas. The flag of France was taken down.

Gist started home in a happy mood. He traveled through the fine forests of the Kentucky bluegrass region, crossed the mountains, and after seven months reported to Lawrence Washington, a member of the Ohio Land Company, at Mount Vernon. Both men were pleased with what Gist had found, but they knew it would not be easy to keep the French out of this country. They were soon proved right.

YOUNG GEORGE WASHINGTON

Washington goes on a dangerous mission and warns the French to leave the Ohio River Valley.

On a crisp October day in 1753, a shy and solemn young man rode his horse down Duke of Gloucester Street in Williamsburg, Virginia. Ducks, geese, and pigs scattered across the road. But George Washington, who was then twenty-one years old, took little notice. His mind was on that duty that had called him to Williamsburg.

The Washingtons were well known in Virginia. George's great-grandfather, John Washington, had reached the colony in 1657, settling in Westmoreland County. George's own birth date was February 22,

Because Washington was a man of courage and strength, and knew how to handle men, Governor Dinwiddie chose him for the task of carrying his note to the French commander in Ohio.

1732, now that Great Britain had adopted the Gregorian calendar and moved the date ahead by eleven days. His boyhood had been spent at Ferry Farm on the Rappahannock River, opposite Fredericksburg.

AT MOUNT VERNON

For George, these happy years had been filled with rowing and fishing and swimming, with riding and hunting in the green hills. His schooling had been incomplete. He knew a little arithmetic, had his own idea of how to spell English words, and could stumble through a printed page as well as the average reader of the period. His father's death, when the boy was eleven, changed his life. In time George's half brother, Lawrence Washington, brought him to live on his estate at Mount Vernon.

To the end of his days George Washington would love this rich, fertile, tidewater country along the Potomac. A well-known man in the region was gruff old Colonel William Fairfax. His disposition was often as prickly as a porcupine, but he took to George. The boy was shy and polite and could ride a horse well—the marks of a gentleman to old Fairfax. He gave George his first job as a surveyor and told him how to invest his money. By the age of eighteen, George was already a landowner and a traveler who had crossed the Blue Ridge Mountains and knew how to get along with frontiersmen and Indians.

Lawrence Washington's health had never been good, and in 1751 he went to the West Indies in the hope that he would grow stronger in the mild climate of the islands.

George Washington almost lost his life in the icebound Allegheny River.

George went with him and came down with the smallpox. The disease left his face marked for the rest of his life.

The climate failed to help Lawrence. Within a few months he was dead, and the management of the estate at Mount Vernon fell to George. From the start, he was equal to the responsibility. Furthermore, he got along well with people, as was shown by his appointment to the rank of major in the Virginia militia.

GOVERNOR DINWIDDIE'S MISSION

George's reputation was growing. Governor Robert Dinwiddie thought highly of him—and that was why on this crisp October day George had come to Williamsburg. Governor Dinwiddie wanted to send him

on a mission, and he did not hide the fact that it was dangerous. The French, who were stringing their forts and trading posts along the Ohio River, continued to dispute British claims to the territory. Occasionally an English frontiersman was driven from his wilderness home. Sometimes he was scalped by an Indian who had drunk too much French brandy. Sometimes he was carried to captivity in Canada. Dinwiddie intended to give the French a stern warning: either stop invading British land along the Ohio or be pushed out.

Carrying this warning to the French was only part of the mission. Washington was also to judge the military strength of French settlements, select sites for British forts, and learn which side the Indians would support in case of war.

Knocked off the raft, he fought his way to a nearby island to recover.

The governor admitted that there might be dangers no one could foresee. No one knew how far the party must travel to reach the French commander. It might be anywhere from 500 to 1,000 miles. The journey would be over strange mountains, through silent forests, and across rushing streams in a country best known for its wild Indians, bears, and rattlesnakes. Winter would bring snow and ice, frozen roads in the valleys and drifts in the mountains. But Washington agreed to do the job, and left that night for Fredericksburg to start organizing his expedition.

WASHINGTON IN THE WILDERNESS

As his guide, Washington chose Christopher Gist. His interpreter was Jacob Van Braam, a Hollander who had taught Washington how to fence. Four Indians who knew the country were also in the party. By late November the little group reached the forks of the Ohio, on the site of present-day Pittsburgh. From there Washington went on into the country of the Delawares.

Dealing with the Indians was a tricky business. Some were friends of the English; others pretended to be friends but could not be trusted. The sly Chabert de Joncaire, son of a French father and a Seneca mother, tried to get the Indians who accompanied Washington to desert him.

But young Washington handled himself well, and by mid-December he had reached Fort Le Boeuf. There he handed Dinwiddie's letter to Legardeur de St. Pierre, the French commandant. St. Pierre treated Washington with great politeness and gave him a reply to carry back to Williamsburg. It told Governor Dinwiddie that St. Pierre intended to do exactly as the French authorities ordered—which was a polite way of saying that if the English wanted to oust the French from the Ohio Valley, they would have to send soldiers and fight a war.

THE HOMEWARD JOURNEY

Gist wondered if Washington had the stamina to make the homeward journey over the mountains and through the snows that fell at this time of year. Gist need not have worried. He would learn that once Washington set himself to a task, he stayed with it until it was finished.

The party traveled on foot most of the way, and once they beat off an attack by Indians. Then, crossing the Allegheny River, cakes of floating ice tipped their raft over. Washington grabbed a raft log and fought his way, half frozen, to a deserted island. Gist now knew the quality of this young fellow.

On May 28, 1754, Washington and his small band of Virginians met the French in the forest near Fort Necessity.

WASHINGTON'S FIRST BATTLE

Washington leads his troops into the wilderness with orders to drive out the French.

When Dinwiddie read St. Pierre's letter, he decided that Virginia must act. Washington, promoted in rank to lieutenant colonel, was placed in charge of raising a militia force. On his suggestion, plans were made to build a fort at the fork of the Ohio and the Monongahela Rivers. In April the Virginians set out with orders to "drive away, kill and destroy, or seize as prisoners all persons not the subjects of the king of Great Britain, who should attempt to take possession of the lands on the Ohio or any of its tributaries."

139

Fort Necessity

The French had also decided to act, as Washington quickly learned in a series of messages from Half King, a friendly Seneca chief. About 1,000 French troops with eighteen cannon had come down the Allegheny to the point where it forks with the Ohio and were occupying the area. Here they were raising a fort named Du Quesne.

Washington's men numbered no more than 150, and he had only a few pieces of light artillery. But he pushed ahead until, late in May, he reached the banks of the Youghiogheny, about forty miles from Fort Du Quesne. A runner from Half King brought him a warning: "Be on your guard. The French are near, and intend to strike the first English whom they see."

A nearby plain, called the Great Meadows, gave Washington a place to make his stand. Here he threw up a stockade, naming it, with grim humor, Fort Necessity. Gist brought further warning that the French had left their tracks within five miles of the Great Meadows. Another runner from Half King informed Washington that the French were waiting in ambush not far off.

A hard rain fell that night. Taking forty men, Washington started out through the darkness to reach Half King's camp, six miles away. Some time after sunrise, after he had been joined by the Indians, Washington led his troops down a trail through a pile of rocks. Suddenly a French sentry appeared. He shouted: "Fire!"

Washington threw his own musket to his shoulder, and in fifteen minutes the battle was over. Ten Frenchmen were killed and twenty-two taken prisoner. Only one Virginian had fallen.

Those fifteen minutes of skirmishing on May 28, 1754, drew first blood in the long and costly French and Indian War. On July 3, a strong French and Indian force stormed down on Fort Necessity in a battle that lasted nine hours. Washington knew that his army was too weak to hold off the foe, and at twilight he agreed to surrender.

Next morning, seated on a log outside the stockade, Washington worked out the terms of surrender with De Villiers, the French commander. The French prisoners must be returned. For a period of one year the Virginians must not try to build a fort west of the mountains. In return, Washington was allowed to lead his troops back home. The French had won the opening round.

BRADDOCK FUMBLES A BATTLE

Refusing to take Washington's advice, Braddock marches his men into a trap set by the French.

In June of 1754, twenty-five delegates from seven colonies met in the old city hall in Albany, New York to try to solve some of their problems. Benjamin Franklin, representing Pennsylvania, came to the meeting with a "Plan of Union" already worked out in his mind. Weeks before, writing in the *Pennsylvania Gazette*, he had spoken sharply of the dangers that would face the colonies unless they agreed upon ways to defend themselves. Beneath a picture of a serpent, divided into as many parts as there were colonies, he had warned: "Join, or Die."

Under Franklin's plan, a grand council or congress would include forty-eight representatives elected by the colonies. Acting within British law, this congress would be responsible for all civil and military affairs. A president general, appointed by the king, would have the power to veto the acts of the congress.

Franklin admitted that his plan was far from perfect, but he felt it was a good start.

Franklin called for the colonies to act together in a cartoon that became famous.

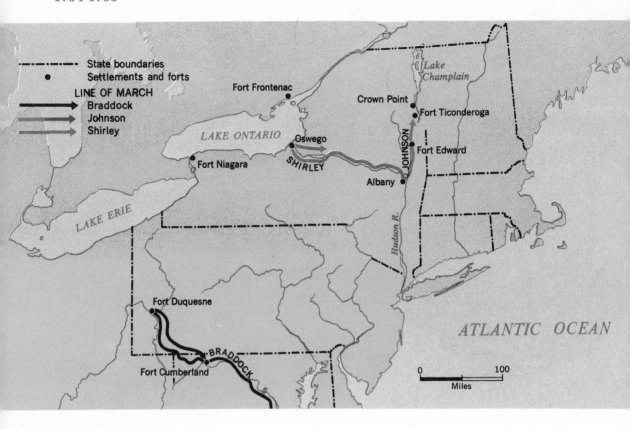

General Braddock planned to send three expeditions against the French and Indians—one led by himself, the others by Governor Shirley of Massachusetts and Sir William Johnson.

No one seemed to like his ideas, however—least of all the authorities in England, who felt his whole scheme was "too democratic."

Yet some plan of co-operation was badly needed. The French were still stirring up the Indians against English settlers in the wilderness. Governor Sharpe of Maryland was placed in temporary command of all colonial forces. Governor Dinwiddie of Virginia paid no attention to him and handled his own forces as he pleased. Unfortunately, Dinwiddie was no military expert. His Virginia militia became so disorganized that Washington threatened to resign his commission.

England then sent two regiments of regular troops to Virginia under the command of Edward Braddock. He was far from a good choice, for he knew nothing about wilderness warfare. In April of 1755, he called the royal governors of Massachusetts, New York, Maryland, North Carolina, Pennsylvania, and Virginia to a meeting in Alexandria, Virginia.

Hard facts had to be faced. Warm weather was approaching, and no one could doubt that the French and the Indians would soon take to the warpath. General Braddock proposed three expeditions to counter the threat.

The first, which he would lead, would strike at Fort Du Quesne. A second force, led by Governor Shirley of Massachusetts, would aim at Fort Niagara at the mouth of the Niagara River, and at Fort Frontenac at the foot of Lake Ontario. A third force, under Sir William Johnson, would seize Crown Point on Lake Champlain.

The British marched through the wilderness as if they were on a parade ground.

Everyone was greatly cheered by Braddock's plan, and all but two colonial legislatures voted to support the coming campaigns. Georgia said it could not spare either men or money. The Quakers of Pennsylvania were opposed to all wars and would not take part in this one.

BRADDOCK'S CONCEIT

Braddock had more conceit than common sense. "The savages may be formidable to your raw American militia," he said to men like George Washington and Benjamin Franklin. "Upon the king's regulars and disciplined troops, it is impossible they should make any impression." When supplies were late in reaching Alexandria, Braddock sometimes raved like a madman.

The American people, he shouted, were without honor, ability, and honesty.

Not until June 19 did Braddock move with his army. The French had been using the time to rally their Indian allies and were more than ready for the British. Washington, who served as an aide to Braddock, commanded the colonial forces in the lead. He wanted to press on and strike quickly, but the cautious British regulars held him back. At last, on July 8, Washington and his Virginians reached the forks of the Monongahela and Youghiogheny Rivers, about a dozen miles from Fort Du Quesne.

The next morning, the British regulars advanced along the southern slopes of the Monongahela. After the fashion of European troops, they marched in neat, solid rows. Washington tried to warn Braddock 143

Just as Washington had predicted, the British regulars were ambushed by the French and Indians.

that this would lead to disaster. There was only one way to fight Indians—in open ranks, man to man. "What!" Braddock said in a burst of anger. "A provincial colonel teach a British general how to fight?"

Refusing to take Washington's advice, Braddock crossed the river and sent his regulars forward in the same solid rows. Under a blistering noonday sun, Braddock and his redcoats plodded on—straight into an ambush. Suddenly bullets and arrows came at them from the woods, while the Indians whooped like demons.

"The Virginia troops showed a good deal of bravery, and were nearly all killed," Washington wrote his mother afterward. "The dastardly behavior of those they call regulars exposed all others, that were inclined to do their duty, to almost certain death. In despite of all the efforts of the officers to the contrary, they ran, as sheep pursued by dogs, and it was impossible to rally them."

Mortally wounded, Braddock was carried from the field. Four bullets pierced Washington's coat and two horses were shot from under him, so that his escape seemed a miracle. But nothing could save the day for the American forces, and they were forced to retreat. Their only good luck was that the French and Indians did not pursue them. Three nights later Braddock was buried by torchlight in the forest, and Washington read the funeral service. Then, wearily, his defeated army began the march toward home.

THE UNHAPPY ACADIANS

*The British force the helpless
Acadians to leave their lands in
Nova Scotia.*

In Nova Scotia during that summer of 1755, the English found an excuse to seize the fertile lands of the Acadians. Roman Catholics who had once refused to take an oath of allegiance were not entitled to a second chance to do so—or so the British authorities decided. This decree made hundreds of innocent families rebels against the king, and their lands were taken away from them.

Despair filled the hearts of the simple Acadians. Some who tried to escape into Canada were hunted down in the woods and shot. An English officer boasted: "Our soldiers hate these French Catholics, and if they can find pretext to kill them, they will." Yet Colonel John Winslow, who was

charged with scattering the Acadians among the English colonies, confessed: "The affair is more grievous to me than any service I was ever employed in."

About 6,000 Acadians were uprooted from their homes. Families were broken up, some never to be reunited. The weeping Acadians were loaded on British ships and dropped along the shores of the Atlantic from the Penobscot to the Savannah Rivers.

In 1755, a British decree declared that the Acadians were rebels, because they had once refused to take an oath of allegiance to the king.

Many wandered off through the forest, going north into Canada or south into Louisiana. Others set out in open boats, hoping to find their way to Europe. Parents searched through the wilderness for their lost children, and the children wandered sadly from one Indian camp to the next in search of their parents. In later years, Henry Wadsworth Longfellow wrote a poem, *Evangeline,* which told the story of these exiles.

BRADDOCK'S PLANS FAIL

Except for this brutal seizure of the Acadians' land, the British had little to show for their first year of struggle with the French and Indians. None of Braddock's three schemes was successful. The expedition against Forts Niagara and Frontenac accomplished very little. The most that could be said for the expedition to Crown Point was that the name of the lake the French called Holy Sacrament was changed to Lake George, in honor of George II, the British king.

The war dragged throughout 1756. The

Earl of Loudon, who was sent to the colonies as commander in chief and governor of Virginia, was a tyrant who talked much and accomplished little. He expected to be obeyed without question, and the more foolishly he acted the less he could stand criticism.

Loudon began an attack against Louisburg, Nova Scotia, then set his troops to cutting down a hill so that he could hold a parade. He waited almost another month while his soldiers planted a vegetable garden. It was no wonder that an officer said one day: "See how the power of England is held in chains by imbecility!" The Indians laughed at the English, calling them "old women." Each month more and more Indians supported the French, who were real soldiers and "acted like men."

FRANCE GAINS POWER

In contrast to Loudon, the French commander, Marquis Louis Joseph de Montcalm de Saint-Véran, knew how to deal with the Indians. When they staged one of their wild war dances, Montcalm danced with them. When they sang their war songs, he sang with them. To the Indians, Montcalm was the sort of general who was worth following.

In 1757 the situation of the English was growing desperate. They had been swept out of the Ohio region, and in northern New York the French and Indians held the upper hand. The French also controlled the St. Lawrence, the Great Lakes, and the valley of the Mississippi. French territory in America was about twenty times greater than that of the British.

The colonies boiled with unrest, and late in the year Bostonians refused flatly to have Loudon's royal soldiers quartered in their city. Loudon acted in his usual way. If the Bostonians did not change their minds in forty-eight hours, he would send troops to force them to obey.

Montcalm ate, danced, and sang with the Indians—and won their respect.

THE TURNING TIDE

Pitt comes to power in England and the colonists raise troops to fight against the French.

But Loudon's days were numbered. In England, William Pitt had risen to power. Never would the American colonists find a warmer, more understanding friend in the British government. Pitt promised the colonies troops, money, and a share in their government. In Sir Jeffrey Amherst, General James Abercrombie, General James Wolfe, and Lord George Howe, he chose able military leaders. When aristocrats in England opened their law books and protested that Pitt was giving the colonies more freedom than the British Constitution intended, he replied: "The lawyers are not to be regarded in questions of liberty."

Confidence spread like a freshening

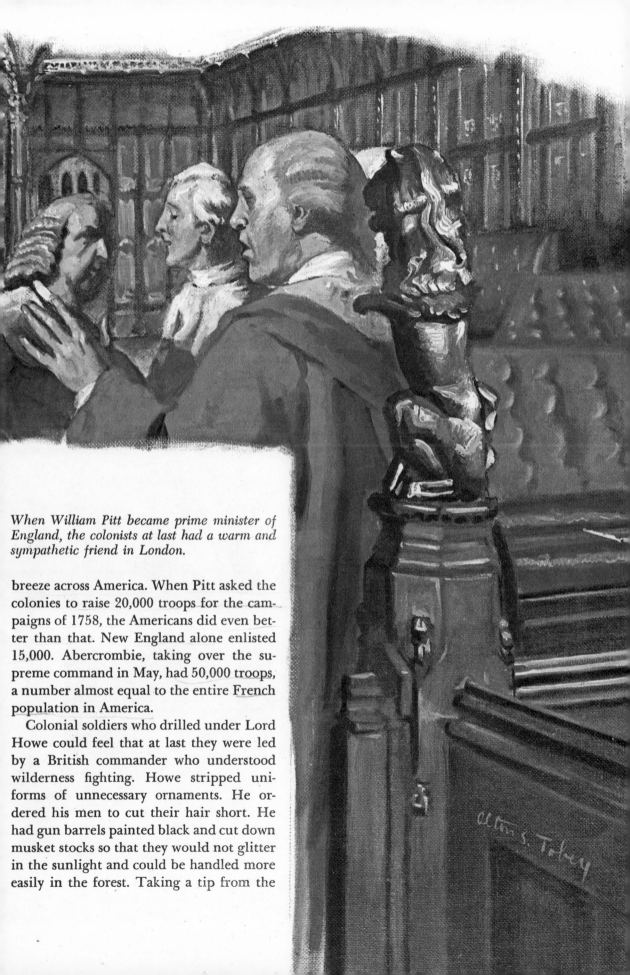

When William Pitt became prime minister of England, the colonists at last had a warm and sympathetic friend in London.

breeze across America. When Pitt asked the colonies to raise 20,000 troops for the campaigns of 1758, the Americans did even better than that. New England alone enlisted 15,000. Abercrombie, taking over the supreme command in May, had 50,000 troops, a number almost equal to the entire French population in America.

Colonial soldiers who drilled under Lord Howe could feel that at last they were led by a British commander who understood wilderness fighting. Howe stripped uniforms of unnecessary ornaments. He ordered his men to cut their hair short. He had gun barrels painted black and cut down musket stocks so that they would not glitter in the sunlight and could be handled more easily in the forest. Taking a tip from the

Indians, he put his men in leggings as a protection against thorns and insects.

In early July more than 1,000 bateaux (tapering, flat-bottomed river craft) and whaleboats carried Abercrombie's army down Lake George. He then marched his troops through the dense forests of the Adirondacks. He planned to attack Fort Ticonderoga, which guarded the natural trade routes between Lakes George and Champlain.

But Ambercrombie's guides were not up to their jobs. Lord Howe, stumbling into an ambush, was killed by a musket ball. With his army in confusion, Abercrombie retreated to re-form his columns.

Within Fort Ticonderoga, Montcalm, with about 4,000 troops, was well prepared for the attack that came on July 8. Abercrombie failed to haul his cannon through the forest—his first mistake. Next he hurled his army against entrenchments too well protected for scaling parties to overcome. At the end of four hours, 2,000 of his soldiers were dead or wounded, and Abercrombie admitted defeat. "What a day for France!" Montcalm wrote afterward. "If I had had two hundred Indians to send out at the head of a thousand picked men . . . not many would have escaped."

Farther south, a British army of about 6,000, including 2,000 Virginians under

Howe simplified weapons and uniforms to adapt them to fighting in the wilderness.

Colonel George Washington, was marching on Fort Du Quesne. General Joseph Forbes, in command of the expedition, was so ill he had to be carried on a litter. Washington advised him to move swiftly by the same route Braddock had taken, but he insisted on building a new road over the Alleghenies. So the army crept rather than marched, and Washington wrote angrily in a letter: "See how our time has been misspent! Behold how the golden opportunity has been lost, perhaps never more to be restored!"

By November, Forbes and his main army were still fifty miles from Fort Du Quesne. Forbes wanted to put off the attack until spring, but Washington disagreed. He had

The British moved slowly down Lake George.

heard that the Indians were growing tired and deserting the French. Now was the time to strike. Forbes gave in and Washington pushed ahead with his brigade. He reached a hill overlooking the fort, where the French had left only 500 troops. That night the French set fire to the fort and fled down the Ohio River in their boats.

WASHINGTON LEAVES FORT PITT

Next day Washington marched in and raised the British flag over the ruins. England now controlled the Ohio basin. The Virginians repaired the fort and renamed it Fort Pitt. Nearby, a little village called Pittsburgh sprang up. Washington, who was now twenty-six years old, marched home determined to leave military life forever. He had other plans. He would take his seat in the Virginia assembly, to which he recently had been elected, and he would marry a charming widow named Martha Dandridge Custis.

153

Wolfe Captures Quebec

The fall of Quebec marks the beginning of the end of French power in America.

William Pitt said that if England wished the co-operation of Americans, "we must be just and allow them freedom." He was a wise statesman, and both the king and Parliament did as he wished.

Now Pitt realized that the victory at Fort Du Quesne meant more than winning the gateway to the West, important as that was.

The Indians were beginning to wonder about their French friends. Perhaps the French were not so powerful as they claimed. This opened up an opportunity to hit hard at the French strongholds of Ticonderoga and Quebec. And once these were conquered, all of North America would be under British control.

THE BRITISH ADVANCE

In 1759 the British forces began a two-pronged movement. One force, under Sir Jeffrey Amherst, moved up Lake Champlain. A second, under James Wolfe, sailed into the St. Lawrence River. The French,

154

Heavily fortified Quebec stood on top of a high hill overlooking the Saint Lawrence River, and was guarded by Montcalm's French troops.

seeing themselves caught like a shell in a nutcracker, retreated from Fort Ticonderoga, and Amherst and his British troops quickly occupied it.

SKIRMISHING FOR QUEBEC

As Wolfe's forces approached Quebec, he must have been concerned at what he saw. The city rose before him on its rock cliff—a neat, tree-shaded community of stone houses, churches, palaces, convents, and gardens. But beyond the city was the loftier height of Cape Diamond. Wherever Wolfe turned, batteries of cannon frowned down upon him. He could also see the tents of Montcalm's army upon the Plains of Abraham, barring the only level approach to the city itself.

The impatient Wolfe was eager for action. The French sent fireboats floating down the Montmorency River, but they were pushed aside before they did any great harm. Wolfe tried to cross the Montmorency and storm the heights to the French camp, but a terrific thunderstorm came up and he was beaten back. When news of this failure reached England, some men said that Wolfe must be mad. "Mad!" King George II said. "Wolfe mad! I wish he'd bite some of the other generals!"

155

Wolfe was a general any king could admire—he was willing to fight. He might make mistakes, but he would learn by his blunders and he would stick to his job. In time, Wolfe would force the battle. He would make Montcalm risk his army.

Long weeks passed as Wolfe thought through his problem. On September 12, 1759, he was ready to move. As evening came on, he raised his wineglass and sang a little army ditty to his staff:

> *Why, soldiers, why*
> > *Should we be melancholy, boys?*
> *Why, soldiers, why,*
> > *Whose business 'tis to die!*

WOLFE STARTS THE ATTACK

Toward nine o'clock that night, Wolfe and his army boarded a fleet of flatboats, floating up the St. Lawrence River with the flood tide. To the French they appeared to be retreating, and cheers rang through the streets of Quebec. But Wolfe had carefully selected the cove where he landed. All at once the English were wading ashore and scrambling up the cliffs, 300 feet above the river. Startled sentries were swept aside. As dawn broke, the French looked upon a scene they could hardly believe. There on the open Plains of Abraham before their city stood 5,000 British troops.

Marching forward to meet his English enemies, Montcalm warned his soldiers: "If it is necessary to fight them, it is necessary to crush them." The two armies were about equal in size when they collided with deadly volleys of muskets. The British stood their ground, then charged with their bayonets.

Standing in the midst of the charge, Wolfe urged his men on. Then he was struck by bullets in the head, abdomen, and breast.

"Support me," Wolfe cried to an officer nearby. "Do not let my brave soldiers see me drop. The day is ours—keep it."

The dying general was led to the rear. An officer shouted, "They run! They run!"

"Who runs?" Wolfe asked feebly.

"The enemy, sir. They give way everywhere."

Wolfe spoke his last words on earth: "Now, God be praised. I die happy!"

QUEBEC SURRENDERS

Wolfe did not know that his brave foe, Montcalm, had also been mortally wounded and would die the next morning. The retreat of the French from the Plains of Abraham doomed Quebec, and five days later the city surrendered. Other campaigns in 1760 completed the British conquest of

Pretending to retreat, Wolfe took his men to a hidden cove, from which they climbed the forbidding cliffs and surprised the French.

The French broke and ran before the British troops, but the brilliant Wolfe was killed at the moment of his greatest victory.

Canada. But before the news could be brought to London, King George II died, at the age of seventy-six.

The war with the French and Indians officially ended with the signing of the Treaty of Paris on February 10, 1763. France ceded to England all claims to territory east of the Mississippi River and north of the latitude of the Iberville River (slightly below Baton Rouge). New Orleans and Louisiana were ceded to Spain. Thus France's dream of a North American empire was brought to an end. By the same treaty, Spain, which had been at war with England, ceded all of Florida to Great Britain. The English claimed, at last, almost half of the continent.

THE REVOLT OF PONTIAC

*An able Ottawa chief stirs up
his people and for a time succeeds
in defeating the British.*

On an April day in 1763, in a meadow near Detroit, many Indian tribes gathered. They included the Ottawas, the Miamis, the Wyandots, the Chippewas, the Potawatomies, the Mississaugues, the Shawnees, the Foxes, the Winnebagoes, and the Senecas. The meeting seemed to be a peaceful one. Children romped at their games, men smoked their pipes, and old squaws exchanged gossip.

But the meeting had another purpose. Pontiac, the great Ottawa chief, rose in war dress and spoke of the danger they all faced from the English. But he had a plan. Cunningly, he described how they could win over the English. They must pretend friendship until they gained admission to British forts. Then they would turn on the English and stain the ground with their blood. The other tribes liked the plan and agreed to go on the warpath with the fierce Pontiac.

Using trickery, he soon captured every post west of Oswego, New York, with the exception of the forts at Niagara, Pittsburgh, and Detroit. A good example of his trickery was what happened at Fort Michillimackinack. Here, on the plain outside the fort, the squaws and braves came daily to play a game of ball. It was exciting to watch, and officers from the fort wandered beyond the gates to see the fun. Suddenly the ball sped toward the fort—and the officers. The braves chased after it. Then the braves turned on the officers, while the squaws threw back their blankets and brought out the hatchets they had been hiding. The Indians soon captured the fort.

THE END OF THE REVOLT

Pontiac's terror spread a bloody trail over a wide area, and British forces set out to put down the Indian revolt. On the last day of July, 1763, they planned to take the Ottawa chief by surprise on the outskirts of Detroit. But it was Pontiac who sprang the surprise, striking the British unexpectedly at a little brook, afterward called Bloody Run. Encouraged by their victories, the Indians carried the war to Detroit and Fort Pitt. There was bitter fighting until the British at last gathered enough men to stop the Indians. Pontiac fled, escaping into the country of Illinois, where he tried to rally other tribes to his cause. It was here that the end came. In 1769, Pontiac attended a celebration in Cahokia, Illinois. During the celebration, an Indian who had been bribed with a barrel of whiskey crept up behind him and killed him with a hatchet.

Pontiac's men tricked the British officers who were watching them play ball, and took the fort. The revolt had begun.

161

ENGLAND TURNS BACKWARD

George III becomes king and chooses advisers who want the colonists to take orders from the government in London.

The young prince who now became King George III of England was popular with the people. He had many difficult problems to solve, and William Pitt offered his help. But the young ruler turned to the Earl of Bute for advice.

A Scottish nobleman, Bute was the king's tutor and favorite companion. He was gay and handsome, but his good qualities seemed to end right there. He had neither the nimble mind of Pitt, nor his feeling for human rights. The result was that England turned backward in its dealings with the

James Otis was cheered in Boston when he spoke against the "writs of assistance," which would permit British agents to enter private homes and shops.

American colonists. Again Americans were treated like distant cousins rather than equal members of the British family.

It was at Bute's suggestion that George III sent secret agents to America to judge the "character" of the colonists. Bute wanted to force Americans to pay taxes to the mother country. His government imposed upon the colonies "writs of assistance." These were court orders that allowed royal agents to enter the shops and houses of Americans to collect taxes.

The writs, first issued in Massachusetts in 1761, stirred up a storm. James Otis, a fiery lawyer, carried the cause of the colonists to a trial in the town hall in Boston. "A man's house is his castle," said Otis. "This writ, if it should be declared legal, would totally annihilate [destroy] this privilege." With such writs, customhouse officers could enter any house they pleased. Otis declared that he would sacrifice "estate, health, applause

and even life" to fight such an unjust law.

When James Otis left the town hall, the people made it clear that they supported him. They cheered and tossed their hats into the air. Although the royal government legalized the issuing of the writs, they were never really enforced.

GRENVILLE REPLACES BUTE

Bute was forced to resign as the King's chief counselor, and George III replaced him with George Grenville. Grenville was Pitt's brother-in-law, but the Americans found that he was no better than Bute. Under Grenville's program, the British House of Commons voted unanimously in 1764 that it had the right to tax the colonists even though they were not represented in Parliament.

The assembly of Massachusetts responded angrily, declaring that "no man can justly take the property of another with- 163

Angered by the Stamp Act, the citizens of New York burned the coach of the tax collector.

out his consent." Thus was born the rallying cry of the next ten years—Americans would never agree to "taxation without representation."

But George III and his counselors had a problem. The French and Indian War had cost a great deal, and Britain badly needed money for the army and navy. Why shouldn't the colonists pay their share? But the colonies could not be depended upon to raise the money themselves. The only way out was to tax the people directly.

And so, in 1764, Grenville suggested the Stamp Act. Americans would be required to put certain stamps on all documents, such as contracts and mortgages, as well as on newspapers and pamphlets. The money paid for the stamps would go to the British government.

Once again the colonists cried out against taxation without representation. The assemblies in Massachusetts, Connecticut, New York, Pennsylvania, Virginia, and South Carolina, each took a firm stand against the Stamp Act. But George III was a stubborn man, who insisted that the Stamp Act must be passed to teach Americans "obedience to the laws and respect for the legislative assembly of the kingdom." By March, 1765, the Stamp Act had passed both houses of Parliament.

THE SONS OF LIBERTY

Strong protests against the Stamp Act cause the king to recall Pitt, and the act is repealed.

No one expected the wave of protest that swept the colonies after the Stamp Act was passed. Groups of men called "Sons of Liberty" were formed in widely scattered towns. Men gathered in taverns, in stores,

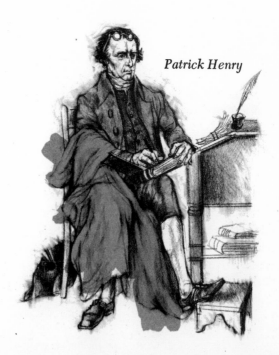

Patrick Henry

and along the roadsides to speak out against the law. Ministers preached against it on Sundays. In Virginia the fiery backwoods statesman, Patrick Henry, shouted that only Americans could tax themselves. Some members of the Virginia House of Burgesses cried, "Treason! Treason!" Henry answered, "If this be treason, make the most of it!"

Agents appointed by England to collect the taxes due under the Stamp Act ran into trouble. In Boston the Sons of Liberty hung an effigy, or dummy figure, of the collector from a large elm called the "Liberty Tree." An angry mob roared: "Death to the man who offers a piece of stamped paper to sell!" Another mob in Providence, Rhode Island, forced the collector to resign, and in New York City the Sons of Liberty burned the collector's coach. In New Jersey, Maryland, Virginia—practically everywhere in the colonies—the same kind of thing was happening.

The Stamp Act took effect on November 1, 1765—a day the colonists called "Black Friday." Church bells rang as though tolling for the death of liberty. 165

Mock funerals paraded through the streets in many cities, towns, and villages. Almost all business was stopped. Rather than buy goods from England, young ladies who called themselves "Daughters of Liberty" met to spin cloth and knit stockings.

PITT SUPPORTS THE COLONIES

In England, George III asked William Pitt to organize a new government. Sick with gout, Pitt hobbled on legs wrapped in flannel to address Parliament. Boldly he declared that, in his opinion, the royal government had no right to tax the colonies without representation. Americans, he said, were "subjects of this kingdom, equally entitled with yourselves to all the natural rights of mankind and the peculiar privileges of Englishmen."

THE STAMP ACT REPEALED

Grenville fought back, calling the colonists rioters on the brink of treason. Pitt spoke against his brother-in-law: "He tells us that America is obstinate—America is in open rebellion. I rejoice that America has resisted. Three millions of people so dead to all the feelings of liberty as to voluntarily submit to be slaves, would have been fit instruments to make slaves of the rest." Pitt

Happy Bostonians met under the Tree of Liberty to celebrate the Stamp Act's repeal.

166

called for the repeal of the Stamp Act, and in March of 1766 Parliament did as he asked.

When the news reached Boston, the Sons of Liberty gathered under their Liberty Tree to celebrate the victory. Bells rang in New York City, and a petition was sent to the assembly to build statues of Pitt and George III. But on both sides of the Atlantic there were some people who wondered how long this patched-up peace between the mother country and the colonies could last. Some Englishmen said the king had been made to bow to his subjects. If this sort of thing were allowed to go on, the British Empire would soon fall apart.

Saving the Liberty Pole

Bad feeling between Bostonians and British troops stationed in the city leads to the Boston Massacre.

William Pitt had been known as the "Great Commoner." When the king made him Viscount Pitt and Earl of Chatham, his popularity dropped sharply. People said that in his old age he was seeking honor and comfort. Pitt's health was failing and he was no longer the real leader of the royal government. Again Parliament forced taxes upon the colonies. This time, if necessary, soldiers would see that the law was obeyed.

New taxes were placed on tea, glass, paper, painters' colors, and various other imports, and a board of tax collectors was set up which was not controlled by colonial assemblies.

TROUBLE IN NEW YORK

Trouble began in the spring of 1767. Troops reaching New York City were jeered by the Sons of Liberty, who had put up a Liberty Pole to show that they were against the taxes. It was torn down by the troops, put up again, and once more hauled down. The Sons of Liberty bound their Liberty Pole with iron to resist the axes of the troops, who loaded their muskets. Only the action of the governor prevented bloodshed. The assembly was forbidden to meet until New Yorkers had a "respectful" attitude toward the royal troops.

A wave of protest rolled across the colonies, just as it had during the days of the Stamp Act. One assembly after another sent petitions to Parliament, whose members began to use words like "rebels," "traitors," and "open revolt." Royal troops were sent to Boston in 1768, and as the months went by, tempers on both sides grew shorter. On 167 a January night in 1770 soldiers cut down Boston's Liberty Pole. They sawed it into small pieces and piled them in front of the meeting place of the Sons of Liberty. Another pole was put up on private property, purchased for that purpose.

Most of the people of Boston had decided not to buy any tea until the tax was removed. One Bostonian who opposed this was Theophilus Lillie, a merchant. He found one day that a mob of small boys had put up a post in front of his store. On it was a crudely carved head and a hand pointing out Lillie's store as a place to avoid. A neighboring merchant named Richardson, whose beliefs were the same as Lillie's, rushed out and tried to pull down the post. When a crowd pelted him with dirt and stones, he lost his head, fled into his store for a musket, and fired into the mob. One boy, Christopher Snyder, was killed and another person was wounded.

Boston made a special occasion of Christopher's funeral. A sign on his coffin read: "Innocence itself is not safe." Almost 1,500 persons marched in the procession to the grave as church bells tolled.

BOSTONIANS RIOT

But worse trouble was brewing. Early March brought a wet snow to Boston, and ice covered the ground. In the twilight, people began to crowd the streets. Some of the men carried clubs and, catching sight of the red-coated troops, they said, "Let's drive out these rascals. They have no business here—drive them out!" Others cried: "Town-born, turn out! Down with the bloody-backs!"

Market stalls were torn down to provide clubs. The soldiers pushed the people aside and ran to their barracks. A barber's boy, recognizing a passing soldier, shouted, "There goes a mean fellow, who will not pay my master for shaving him." A sentinel knocked down the boy with his musket.

THE BOSTON MASSACRE

The whole city seemed stirred up. Men were marching on the customhouse on King Street when the barber's boy said, "There's the scoundrel who knocked me down!" Angry voices shouted, "Let us knock *him* down. Down with the bloody-backs! Kill him! Kill him!"

The crowd threw snowballs and pieces of ice at the sentinel, who ran up the steps of the customhouse and called for help. Soldiers appeared, and more snowballs were thrown. A mulatto from Nantucket named Crispus Attucks rallied the mob with wild shouts: "Come on! Don't be afraid!" they cried, "They daren't fire! Kill 'em!"

He rushed forward, struggling to seize a soldier's musket. The soldier fired his gun and Attucks fell dead. Five other soldiers began shooting. Three men were killed and eight more wounded, and the crowd swiftly melted away.

Soon alarm bells were ringing, and drums beat out the call to arms. The streets echoed to the exciting cry: "The soldiers are murdering the people! To arms! To arms! Turn out with your guns!" But there was no more bloodshed. A British captain and eight soldiers were arrested and jailed on charges of murder.

Men like Samuel Adams and John Hancock, who wanted the colonists to break away from English rule, made the most of what happened that day. They called it the

Angry Bostonians jeered at the red-coated British troops, calling them "lobster-backs."

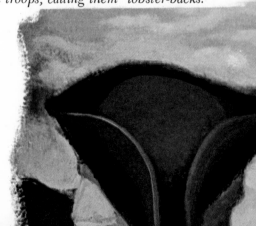

In Boston on March 5, 1770, British soldiers fired on a rioting mob. The colonists called it "the Boston Massacre."

Boston Massacre, and they saw that the news was carried to every colony. They distributed an engraving made by Paul Revere, which showed British redcoats firing on defenseless Americans. John Adams, who one day would be President of the United States, later wrote that never was an event in American history more important "than the battle of King Street, on the 5th of March, 1770. The death of four or five persons, the most obscure and inconsiderable that could have been found upon the continent, has never yet been forgiven in any part of America."

To John Adams, however, and to Josiah Quincy, Jr., fell the task of defending Captain Preston and his soldiers against the charge of murder. Adams and Quincy had strong personal feelings, but as lawyers they carried out their duties as well as they could. Preston and six of the soldiers were declared not guilty. The other two, convicted of manslaughter, were branded on the hand with a hot iron.

THOMAS JEFFERSON IN WILLIAMSBURG

Jefferson attends William and Mary College and shows a knowledge of law and a passion for justice.

No one understood more clearly than John Adams what was happening in America. "The Revolution was effected before the war commenced," he said in later years. "The Revolution was in the minds and hearts of the people." There was another man who also recognized this fact, and who followed John Adams as President of the United States. He was Thomas Jefferson.

Jefferson was seventeen, a rail of a boy standing over six feet, when he arrived in Williamsburg, Virginia, to enroll as a student at William and Mary College. He had hair the color of a carrot, and with his bony arms and spindlelegs he made quite a sight jogging down Duke of Gloucester Street for his daily exercise.

But Jefferson had a mind of his own and was interested in everything that went on around him. He often studied fifteen or sixteen hours a day, and soon he was at the top of his class. Even more important, he attracted the attention of George Wythe.

JEFFERSON STUDIES LAW WITH GEORGE WYTHE

Wythe, whose name rhymes with Smith, was the first professor of law in America. He would count many famous men among his students—men like Henry Clay, Chief Justice John Marshall, and Edmund Randolph. But his favorite was Jefferson, who began to study under him about 1762. Never were teacher and student better suited to each other. Both had brilliant minds, a love for people, a sense of justice. And both were strong-willed, a fact that brought them into court one day on opposite sides of a famous trial.

The belief that the law should protect human rights led Jefferson to take the case of a young mulatto boy named Sam Howell. In Virginia the law said that a child born of a slave woman was also a slave. But Sam was the grandson of a slave, and Jefferson said that there was a law above the law of Virginia. This higher law, under which "all men are free," came from God. Jefferson spoke boldly to the frowning judge: "So that the position as first laid down is proven, that the act of 1705 makes servants of the first mulatto, that of 1723 extends it to her children, but that it remains for future legislation, if any shall be found wicked enough, to extend it to the grandchildren."

As Jefferson expected, he lost the case.

172

Thomas Jefferson

But he had come to grips with an important principle. Before long, that principle would be stated in the Declaration of Independence as: "All men are created equal."

George Wythe was only one of the men with whom Jefferson formed warm friendships while he was in Williamsburg. Among them were Patrick Henry, George Washington, Edmund Pendleton, Richard Henry Lee, and George Mason.

In 1765 Jefferson heard Patrick Henry speak out against the Stamp Act. He was in the crowd that jeered at the tax collector, who left Williamsburg as quickly as possible. In the spring before the Boston Massacre, Jefferson was a member of the Virginia House of Burgesses that opposed the new taxes ordered by the royal government. With other citizens of Williamsburg, he had stared angrily at Paul Revere's engraving of the Boston Massacre. And so Jefferson came to know the men and events that helped to shape the future of the country.

After setting fire to the Gaspee, *Whipple and his men returned to shore.*

THE GASPEE AFFAIR

A British schooner sent to stop smuggling is lured onto a sand bar and burned.

To avoid paying the taxes on imported goods, some of the colonists turned to smuggling. A favorite place for smugglers was Narragansett Bay in Rhode Island, and in March, 1772, the British decided to do something about it. They sent an armed schooner, the *Gaspee,* under the command of Lieutenant Dudingston, to patrol the bay. Dudingston liked power and did not hesitate to use force. His actions outraged the Rhode Islanders, and John Adams said, "His brutal, hoggish manners are a disgrace to the royal navy and the king's service."

One of Dudingston's orders was that all packet ships must lower their flag as a sign of respect when they passed the *Gaspee.* On

The news that tea would be sold directly to the colonists made American tempers rise.

June 9, the packet *Hannah* failed to lower her flag, and Dudingston set out after her. But the tide was going out, and the crew of the *Hannah* maneuvered their ship so as to mislead the *Gaspee*. Suddenly the British schooner was scraping bottom, hopelessly grounded.

THE "GASPEE" IS BURNED

News of the *Gaspee* quickly spread through the nearby city of Providence. The excited colonists saw that here was their chance to rid themselves of Dudingston. That night, sixty-four armed men, commanded by Captain Abraham Whipple, took their places in eight boats and rowed out to the *Gaspee*. Dudingston was wounded by a shot from one of Whipple's men. Boarding the *Gaspee,* the colonists put the crew on shore and set the ship afire. When the flames reached the powder magazine, there was a tremendous explosion—and that was the end of the *Gaspee*.

WALLACE AND WHIPPLE

The furious British offered $5,000 for the capture of the leader of the Providence rebels. In time, they discovered Whipple's part in the affair, and a British admiral sent him a sharp note:

You, Abraham Whipple, on the 10th of June, 1772, burned his majesty's vessel, the Gaspee, *and I will hang you at the yard-arm.*

James Wallace.

The captain replied good-humoredly:

Sir,—Always catch a man before you hang him.

Abraham Whipple.

Tea and "Mohawks"

The arrival of shiploads of British tea in Boston harbor angers Bostonians and leads to the Boston Tea Party.

The refusal of Americans to buy tea was costing the British money. The warehouses of the East India Company were piled high with about 17,000,000 pounds of tea that could not be sold, and in 1773 the company asked the royal government for help. The government agreed that the company's agents could sell the tea directly to the people of the colonies, instead of to the merchants. That way the tea would sell at a much lower price, the Americans would rush to buy such a bargain, the government would collect its tax, and the East India Company would be saved.

But as the ships carrying the tea approached the harbors of the colonies, it became clear that there would be no rush to buy. The merchants were angry because they would get no share of the profits, the smugglers had tea of their own to sell, and the ordinary colonist would not buy goods that had been taxed without his consent.

In New York City there was a meeting to thank those "patriotic" merchants who refused to handle the tea. In Philadelphia a large gathering of people in the yard of the State House cheered the declaration that the action of the East India Company was "a violent attack upon the liberties of America." Charleston stood firmly against doing business with the tea-ships. And on November 29, the following notice was posted throughout the city of Boston:

"Friends! Brethren! Countrymen!—That worst of plagues, the detested *tea,* shipped

Next page: *Disguised as Mohawks, Boston patriots threw the British tea into Boston harbor.* 177

At his Virginia home, Jefferson gave much thought to the problems facing the colonies.

for this port by the East India Company, is now arrived in the harbor. The hour of destruction, or manly opposition to the machinations [plots] of tyranny, stares you in the face. Every friend to his country, to himself and to posterity [his descendants], is now called to meet at *Faneuil Hall,* at nine o'clock THIS DAY (at which time the bells will ring), to make united and successful resistance to this last, worst, and most destructive measure of administration."

THE BOSTON TEA PARTY

The feeling in Boston rose, and on December 16 it boiled over. That evening a town meeting was told that the governor of Massachusetts had refused to send away the tea-ships. Samuel Adams then said that the meeting could do nothing more to save the country, and there was a shout from the gallery: "Boston harbor a teapot tonight! Hurrah for Griffin's Wharf!" As soon as the meeting ended, a number of men, many disguised as Mohawk Indians, hurried through the bright, cold, moonlit night toward Griffin's Wharf. One of them was George Hewes, who later wrote:

"When we arrived at the wharf, there were three of our number who assumed an authority to direct our operations, to which we readily admitted [agreed]. They divided us into three parties, for the purpose of boarding the three ships that contained the tea at the same time. . . . The commander of the division to which I belonged, as soon as we were on board the ship, appointed me boatswain, and ordered me to go to the captain and demand of him the keys to the hatches and a dozen candles. . . . We then were ordered by our commander to open the hatches, and take out all the chests of tea and throw them overboard, and we im-

mediately proceeded to execute his orders, first cutting and splitting the chests with our tomahawks, so as thoroughly to expose them to the effects of the water. In about three hours . . . we had thus broken and thrown overboard every tea chest to be found. . . ."

It was, George Hewes remembered, the "stillest night" Boston had known for several months. Onlookers who tried to snatch up small parcels of tea for their own use had them knocked out of their hands. One old fellow, who tried to hide the tea in his hat, was turned upside down and lost tea, hat, and wig in a single shake. When daylight broke, the harbor was afloat with tea.

JEFFERSON SHOCKS HIS FRIENDS

Too ill to be a delegate, Jefferson writes down some ideas for the Virginia Assembly to discuss and pass on to the Continental Congress.

When word of the Boston Tea Party reached Williamsburg, many people nodded their heads in approval. On June

1, 1774, George III and his counselors punished the Bostonians by closing the city's port. Word of this, too, reached Williamsburg, and Virginians observed a day of prayer to show their sympathy for their fellow colonists in Massachusetts. Stubborn George III and his advisors never seemed to understand that their treatment of the colonies was driving them to act together in common defense. And each act carried them a step closer to breaking with Britain and forming a new nation.

That summer a call went out for all the colonies to send delegates to a continental congress that would meet in Philadelphia in September. Every colony but Georgia responded promptly. Thomas Jefferson had many ideas he wished to place before the Virginia delegates to the congress. But he was too ill to leave his home at the time, so he sent a long document to Williamsburg.

Jefferson's ideas shocked some of his friends. He listed the colonies' grievances against the king and his Parliament. Among them were restrictions on trade, unfair taxes, the dissolving of representative bodies of government, and the sending of armed troops. Jefferson warned the king:

"Open your breast, Sire, to liberal and expanded thought. Let not the name of George the third be a blot in the page of history."

And he also said, "The whole art of government consists in the art of being honest."

Day by day, America was drawing closer to the victory that must come first if ever it would be free—the victory which John Adams described so well and which could only be won within the minds and hearts of the people.

THE NEXT VOLUME IN THIS SERIES

VOLUME

3

THE AGE OF REVOLUTION

Volume III, The Age of Revolution, *begins with
the closing of the port of Boston by the British
as punishment for the Boston Tea Party. It goes on
to describe the mounting bitterness that led to the
Battle of Lexington and the Revolution.
Many people played important roles in America's
fight for freedom. There were heroes and bunglers
and even traitors in those times that tried men's
souls, as well as the soldiers who were simply trying
to win the war so that they could live as they pleased
in their own country.*
The Age of Revolution *tells the
story of their battles, their retreats, their hardships,
until victory at Yorktown allowed
a new nation to come into being.*
The Age of Revolution *covers the years 1774-1783.*